Twelve Positive Habits of
Spiritually Centered People

Other Books by Mark Thurston

Twelve Positive Habits of Spiritually Centered People

By Mark Thurston
and
Sarah Thurston

ARE PRESS

ASSOCIATION FOR
RESEARCH AND
ENLIGHTENMENT

A.R.E. Press • Virginia Beach • Virginia

A.R.E. Press
215 67th Street
Virginia Beach, VA 23451-2061

Thurston, Mark, A.
    Twelve positive habits of spiritually centered people / by Mark Thurston, and Sarah Thurston.
        p.   cm.
    ISBN 0-87604-428-3
    1. Spiritual life. 2. Cayce, Edgar, 1877-1945. 3. Association for Research and Enlightenment. I. Thurston, Sarah, 1981- II. Title.
BP605.A77   T49   2001
131—dc21

                                                    2001002112

Cover design by Richard Boyle

Dedication

To our friend Joe Dunn. As Publisher of A.R.E. Press, Joe enthusiastically supported the idea of this book from its initial proposal. And as a dear friend, he has inspired us with his positive spirit and his courage in all that life has brought his way.

Contents

Introduction

Simple Habits, Powerful Results

You know the feeling: too busy to do what you know you ought to be doing. It's so easy to get caught up in the busyness of the world. And when that happens, spiritually centering activities are squeezed out. You don't find time for a rejuvenating walk in nature or the quiet time to read something inspirational.

It's a fact of modern life that time is at a premium for most people. Sometimes we may find ourselves asking, "How long will it take?" before we ask, "And what will it cost?" Extraordinary stress is created when we feel like there're just not enough hours in the day to do what needs to be done.

Most of us find that when time is tight, life-affirming disciplines easily get overlooked or skipped. Perhaps there's little or no time in the morning to think about your dreams, let alone write them down. When life is hectic you may not do a very good job following the nutritional rules that you know are best. And meditation periods—which ideally take fifteen, twenty, or more minutes of quality, stress-free attention—are forgotten or brushed aside.

Wouldn't it be great if spiritual and psychological benefits could be reaped from even *brief* investments of time and attention? How might your life be transformed by *simple, positive habits* that could keep you spiritually connected? Edgar Cayce, one of the most important spiritual philosophers of the twentieth century, had recommendations for exactly how you can do it.

Cayce made his reputation as a healer—a man whose clairvoyant insights and natural remedies earned him fame as one of the founders of the holistic healing movement. But his remarkable prescriptions usually weren't just herbal tonics, dietary changes, or nontraditional therapies. Frequently Cayce saw that the source of an ailment was a profound stress within the soul—a serious imbalance in lifestyle.

The people who came to him were individuals in the midst of suffering—be it physical, mental, or spiritual. They were dealing with the tensions and uncertainties of life in the Depression years and World War II, surely times of stress at least as great as our own overcharged, hurried era. Cayce offered each individual a program of positive habits that was designed to turn their lives around and get them recentered on what really counts. *The same positive habits can work for people today.*

The basic strategy of this book is to re-create the best of what Cayce had to say to people who sought a healthy, spiritually centered way of life. It's a set of twelve positive habit patterns for balanced living—simple methods that take only small investments of time and energy, wisely used. That impact is nothing less than

- renewed vitality,
- a deeper sense of meaning, and
- a stronger connection to our creative Source.

Of course, some would say that all habits work against spiritual development—that the work of soul growth is really all about becoming more conscious, and so anything that is done habitually is counterproductive. But if we look more closely at the nature of personal transformation, we'll see that there really *is* a place for constructive, life-affirming "habits." That means patterns of thinking, feeling, and acting that are done on a regular basis and serve to awaken us.

Here is an outline of twelve positive habits for modern-day, busy people who want to stay spiritually centered. These twelve patterns for living are examined in detail through the chapters of this book.

Positive Habit #1: Start the Day Right

The *first minute* of our waking day contains a potent opportunity. We set in motion a tone for the day by our mental orientation in those first sixty seconds. This chapter introduces the concept of personality and individuality. Much of the stress and discord in our lives comes from confusing these two sides of ourselves.

This chapter prescribes a direct method to affirm and connect with the individuality in the first minute of the day. In so doing, we make the transition from sleep to wakefulness one in which we're most likely to have a centered, stress-reduced day ahead.

Positive Habit #2: Three-Minute Meditation

Although more lengthy meditations offer many additional rewards, even meditation sessions as short as three minutes can produce clear, positive results. This chapter describes the basics of how to meditate, along with specific suggestions for how to get the most from mini-meditation periods. Even on the busiest, most hectic day, there's usually time for a three-minute meditation, and it can have tremendous value.

Positive Habit #3: The Inner Witness: Practicing Self-Observation

Many spiritual philosophies have taught that people in everyday life are oblivious to reality. We are "hypnotized" as some great teachers (such as Plato in the allegory of

"The Cave") have suggested. We are "asleep" as other teachers have claimed. The secret to waking up and becoming creative and vital is to practice the habit of self-observation. A life-changing effect can occur with this simple technique, done three times daily for even a minute at a time.

Self-observation (or "learning to stand aside and watch self go by" as Cayce described the process) is a practiced skill that brings forth a new kind of attention. A remarkable new sense of oneself begins to grow—a way of knowing ourselves that is detached from any problem, crisis, or worry. This method is the habit of occasionally being an inner witness to our own thoughts, emotions, and deeds. With simple instruction this potent habit can be learned and immediately put to work to transform our lives.

Positive Habit #4: The Pace of Life

Each of us can find an ideal pace for life. But establishing that positive habit starts with self-awareness. Observe yourself. Does life feel slow paced with inertia, idleness, or fatigue? Or, on the other hand, does your life feel rushed and tense, maybe with the sense that you'll never get done all the things you've expected of yourself that day? For most of us, there are strong patterns as we slip into one extreme or the other.

With careful attention and right effort we can adopt an optimal pace for living. It allows relaxation and peace. But at the same time we find a way to get things done with right timing.

Positive Habit #5: Balanced Living

Life is a continual tug-of-war between competing opposites within ourselves. The trick is to develop the creative habit for finding the equilibrium point—the place of balance. This chapter explores balance from many perspectives, starting with nutrition. Cayce had a specific formula for a stress-reducing diet with the key being a particular balance between acid-metabolizing foods and alkaline-metabolizing ones.

Another essential ingredient to this positive habit for balance concerns self-interest versus interest-in-the-needs-of-others. Either extreme is sure to be a stress builder in the long run. To create a tension-free life one must find the point of equilibrium between inner growth and service. This chapter examines specific ways in which one can hold on to both sides in this pair of opposite impulses and achieve a healing synthesis.

Positive Habit #6: Self-Assertion and Healthy Will

Many of our stresses come from a simple fact: we don't understand or make positive use of our free will. Cayce often stated clearly that the right use of will was the pivotal factor in getting one's life on track. The failure to follow this positive habit is an invitation to an array of disappointments and frustrations.

One special point of emphasis in this chapter is the proper application of self-assertion. In his spiritual advice to troubled, unhappy people, Cayce sometimes advocated increased self-assertion. However, that positive habit wasn't an invitation to aggressive, self-serving behavior. Its true, life-centering potential depends upon a correct understanding of the quality of the human soul called free will.

Positive Habit #7: Picture Yourself: Using Creative Visualization for Change

The human mind is an extraordinary tool for change, and change is often the key to shaping a spiritually centered life. Anything about ourselves that we want to transform is within our reach if we use the mind skillful. One powerful method is the creative use of visualization. If specific mental imagery is linked to a clear motivation and purpose, then physical life responds. Cayce often prescribed visualization as a powerful tool for the reduction of stress and for the promotion of healing. This chapter will explore specific ways to practice creative imagery, as well as outline things to avoid when making use of this potent method.

Positive Habit #8: Tolerance: The Magic Ingredient in Human Relationships

Many of us find that the single most difficult aspect of living is human relations. If we could solve the riddle of getting along with people, the ideal of a spiritually centered life would be within reach.

In describing a positive habit to transform our relationships, Cayce pointed to one attitude above all others as the key: tolerance. In essence, tolerance is the face of love. It is the way that we give other people the freedom to be themselves, while at the same time deepening relationships through caring. This chapter takes a careful look at what tolerance really is (and what it is not). Practical hints point the way toward making this attitude the natural and immediate habit in every one of our relationships.

Positive Habit #9: The Sixth Sense in Sleep

Much of what knocks us off center is our confusion and the need for reliable answers. People who came to Cayce for advice were often tension-filled because of their inability to get solutions to everyday problems. Those tensions and stresses sometimes became an even bigger problem in and of themselves, leading to a host of physical ailments. But Cayce encouraged the development of a positive habit to tap into one's own innate ability to get reliable answers, especially through a so-called sixth sense that lives (usually unconsciously) within us all.

Each night as we fall asleep, our minds shift gears and begin to make use of the sixth sense. This additional perceptual ability is highly intuitive. It can tune-in to other people and operate telepathically. It can perceive likely events of the future. In addition, this sixth sense can tap creative wisdom and resources of one's own higher self. One direct way in which we experience this extended sense is in our dreams; *but* it is active all night long and isn't confined just to dreaming. This chapter will describe how the sixth sense works and give instructions for simple ways to become more alert to the valuable information it can provide daily.

Positive Habit #10: Keeping Daily Rhythms

In a world that often seems fast-paced and hectic, what can we do if we want to maintain healthy, balanced lives? What can counteract the many influences that throw us off kilter, disorient us, and drain our energies? Often it's the unpredictability of life that exhausts us. Things happen that weren't part of what we expected. Too easily a day can become disjointed, and we can end up feeling as if circumstances are in control, instead of our being in control of them. The positive habit of creating a daily rhythm can begin to make a big difference.

Rhythms are a close cousin to cycles. Both involve the regular occurrence of certain influences or activities. They are dependable, positive patterns in life. They remind us that we live in an orderly universe.

This chapter will focus on a daily rhythm that Cayce frequently prescribed: "After breakfast work awhile, after lunch rest awhile, and after dinner walk a mile." The reader will be invited to adapt that formula to his or her own lifestyle, then make a commitment to that rhythm as a life-centering pattern.

Positive Habit #11: The Three-Step Body Tuneup

Here's a positive habit from Cayce that focuses directly on health practices which promise to transform us. These three simple methods take only a few minutes a day and minimal effort, but they have led to big changes for many people. First is adequate intake of water. Second is an easy head-and-neck exercise that helps reduce the tension and stress that we store in our neck and shoulders. Third is an exercise in attentive eating for one meal per day. Taken together as a three-step body tuneup, this positive habit is Cayce's most easily applicable set of physical recommendations for reestablishing a centered life.

Positive Habit #12: Wrapping Up the Day: Bedtime Imaginative Recall

Just as Positive Habit #1 dealt creatively with the first waking moments of each day, Positive Habit #12 focuses on the final two or three minutes. The positive habit is to go back through the events of the day and observe in one's imagination the impact of one's deeds, words, and thoughts. Properly done, this review is completed with a spirit of objective love rather than with any sense of guilt or criticism. By consciously taking note of the lessons learned and the intentions left unfulfilled, we are likely to find a deeper and more restful sleep. And we may also find ourselves better equipped to meet the challenges of the new day.

Exploring these twelve positive habits of spiritually centered people is actually an adventure that can be undertaken in any order. Each chapter of the book—each positive habit—is presented in a stand-alone fashion and you can feel free to read the chapters in whatever order appeals to you. The key, though, is to apply the ideas. The habit works only if you'll put attention and energy into letting it work its magic on you.

*Positive
Habit
#1*

Start the Day Right

Starting off on the right foot. Making a good first impression. Getting out of bed on the right side. Our language is full of expressions that convey the same message: the way we *begin* something has a big impact.

In fact, the first sixty seconds of your day may be the most important. In those initial moments you set in motion patterns that will subtly shape your experiences for many hours to come. That start-up programming can be conscious and purposeful, or—as it usually occurs for most people—it can be automatic and haphazard. The difference has a lot to do with whether or not your day unfolds as a centered and healthy one. In fact, here's the very best place to start creating a spiritually centered life.

Waking up in the morning is a turning point. You move from the realm of sleep and dreams back into your familiar world of busy activity and responsibility. And the *way you go through* that turning point—the way you make that transition—may be much more influential than you realize.

Waking up in the morning is a crossroads. Something special happens in that simple act of emerging from sleep and regaining normal consciousness. Profound influences are set in motion by the way in which you make the transition from one dimension of awareness to another. However, before creating an optimal plan for the use of that first minute in the morning, it's worth examining more carefully what's at work here.

Whenever we make a change in consciousness—any dramatic shift in our level of awareness—very important factors come into play. The quality and content of the experiences that follow are largely shaped by *what is held in mind during the transition*. This is not an abstract principle of psychology. It's something we can observe every day, especially by looking carefully at nighttime experiences.

What happens to us during sleep (in dreams and otherwise) is heavily influenced by our state of mind as we drift off at night. You've probably encountered this principle in both negative and positive ways. For example, if you're worried or upset when you go to bed, you're likely to have a troubled night's sleep. On the other hand, if you drift off with a question on your mind, you may well get an answer to that very issue through your dreams.

A similar process is at work for the transition we call death. Research with so-called "near-death experiences" suggests that the attitudes and feelings of the dying individual play a major role in the types of experiences that the soul will have immediately upon passing over. According to this theory, experiences after death eventually transcend what was on the dying person's mind, but *initially* they are especially influential.

A rather mysterious biblical passage hints at all this—a short teaching from the book of Ecclesiastes (11:3). "As a tree falls, there shall it lie." What's the hidden meaning in that enigmatic statement? The fall of the tree represents the transition. Its orientation for that fall—be it north, south, east, or west—establishes the direction in which it will lie on the ground for a long time to come. In the same way, our inclinations and propensities at the time of a change play a big part in shaping our experiences thereafter.

Getting back to the idea of waking in the morning, let's consider what goes on at the time of that transition. Many sources of wisdom believe that during the night we leave our bodies. We "travel" in other dimensions of consciousness. In fact, we might understand sleep to be somewhat like the after-death state. It's almost as if each time we fall asleep we rehearse what it will be like to die. The main difference is that we retain connections to our physical bodies which allow us to come back in the morning. We are psychologically born again at the beginning of each day as we move from one level of consciousness outside of our bodies back to the familiar level of physical awareness.

Most of us never stop to notice very carefully the flow of thoughts and feelings first thing in the morning. Our inner life just sort of "happens," as if it were on automatic pilot. And so, we miss a powerful opportunity to shape the quality of the day that lies ahead.

What *is* the nature of our typical early morning thought patterns? For many people it concerns all the expectations and demands of the day. They wake up and immediately begin to think (or worry) about everything that must be accomplished in the next fourteen to eighteen hours. That automatic agenda hardly leaves any breathing space. What's more, it often pops up almost before we can clear our eyes and begin to think straight.

For other people the first minute or two in the morning is a time to daydream lazily—to drift off in fantasies of what they wish they had in life, imaginings that quickly dissipate once they have to face the realities of the world a few minutes later.

One way to understand what goes on in our minds is to consider two sides of our own psychology. Cayce referred to one aspect as the *personality;* the other, the *individuality.* Briefly, the personality is that part of us that operates primarily on automatic pilot. It is the side of us that others see and know—the facade or persona, we might say. On the other hand, the individuality is the more authentic spiritual self. Without it, we're really nothing. It is the "higher self," an expression that's become popular in recent years. It's the individuality that surfaces when we meditate successfully. In fact, one way to define meditation is an activity that partakes, not of the personality, but of the individuality.

Even though the individuality is clearly the superior element in us, the personality has a constructive role to play as well, *if* it will agree to limit its authority. Instead of usurping leadership, its place is to serve the individuality and the high purposes within the soul. Unfortunately, the personality tends to do otherwise. It wants to be in charge. It has its own agenda and desires, and the personality tries to take control whenever it can.

One of the most distinct characteristics of the personality is a false notion of itself. In other words, we all have certain ideas about ourselves that are illusory. Those distortions come in many shapes and sizes, including:

- exaggerated notions of our own importance—what we might call self-aggrandizement;
- overly critical ideas about our own shortcomings—what we might call self-condemnation;
- distorted pictures of who and what we are supposed to become—expectations that don't come from our own individualities but instead from parents, friends, or the society at large.

What does all this have to do with how you wake up in the morning? Simply this: *Unless you make a conscious effort to do otherwise, your personality self quickly gains control of your life first thing in the morning.* Unless you use your free will to change the pattern, the habitual thoughts and feelings of your personality self grab your attention from the initial minutes of the day. And in so doing, chances are severely diminished that your individuality will awaken and provide direction during the day. This condition is a sure-fire formula for tension and stress in the day that lies ahead.

What does it feel like when your personality makes this grab for power? You may experience it as a burden—the weight that comes from having a mental list of ways you have to please everyone else in your life today. Or, you may feel it as worry when you consider all the problems that you're sure to face in the hours ahead. Another possibility is that first thing in the morning your personality will make you feel frustrated or discouraged, almost wishing that you didn't have to get up because your actual life situation is so far removed from what you desire.

What's the remedy? Transition times are especially important, so it's crucial to get the day started right with a positive habit. But the question remains, "*How* can I, at least temporarily, keep my personality from asserting itself and instead let my individuality set a tone for the day?"

Here's the creative habit that can make the difference. Its essence is *a prayerful attitude that invites spiritual guidance*. First thing in the morning upon awakening, you can dedicate one minute to God. If worries, concerns, to-do-lists, or desires try to squeeze in, they can be gently but firmly instructed to wait. No doubt they will get their turns later, but for this first minute of the day—as the transition is being completed back to physical consciousness—an expression of the individuality self will be given top priority.

Here's one way to prayerfully hold that attitude. When you first wake up in the morning, say silently to yourself, "God, what would *You* have me do today." Repeat it several times, and do it with sincerity. It's crucial that you really mean it. Feel your openness to be guided. Then listen for an inner response—an intuitive prompting or an inner knowing about what's important for the day ahead.

Let your individuality self function clearly and be intuitively receptive. Let yourself be inspired with a sense of what the top priority for the day ought to be.

Of course, this is no magic incantation, and you can certainly reword the prayer if an adaptation fits you better. But no matter what exact words you choose, remember that it's not merely a matter of saying the words by rote, just to get it over with. The power of the words comes *when your mind sincerely feels their meaning.* As you say the prayer, you've got to really mean it! A feeling of trust and surrender is required, a willingness to believe that God has a way that *this very day* can best be lived.

Notice something about the suggested format, "God what would *You* have me do this day?" These words are in the form of a question, so this morning habit doesn't end with a sincere repetition of the words. The listening that follows is vital.

And what kind of a response can be expected? A few people have reported a still small voice that gives guidance for the day: an attitude to hold in mind, the reminder of a specific person to help, or a project to start. More often people who have tried this exercise get a different result. They hear no voice—audible or from within—but instead they receive a clear impression about how to meet the day. It may come as an intuition about the best way to face challenges that will arise. Or, it may come as an inspiration to take some initiative.

Other people have found that nothing comes to them in those early morning moments. They repeat the words of surrender and openness, they listen inwardly and outwardly, but nothing seems to happen. Nevertheless, these same individuals have found that something has qualitatively shifted by having started out the day this way. They find that the basic attitude of trust and openness carries over. Perhaps the guidance comes later in the day. Even though the personality self quickly asserts its agenda upon getting out of bed, still the day goes differently than it might have because of that questioning prayer—"God, what would *You* have me do this day?"

A STORY FROM THE CAYCE ARCHIVES

One of the best illustrations of this prescription from Edgar Cayce—to start the day right—comes from the story of a sixty-one-year-old woman. Agnes made the long train ride to Virginia Beach in the second week of May. It was 1943, and as they came into the Norfolk and Virginia Beach area it was evident that this was a center of wartime activity.

But it wasn't to see mighty naval ships or watch fighter aircraft making practice flights that brought her on this lengthy trip. She had an appointment for May 16 with a most unusual man. Almost everything she knew of Edgar Cayce was from her friend Martha, who had invited her and two other friends to make this venture. The four women were coming to get psychic readings and personal advice from Cayce—hopefully with as much success as Martha had already had getting medical counsel from Cayce for her arthritis.

Agnes' needs, however, weren't related to physical health. She was troubled by the tensions of uncertainty. Recently widowed, she was confused about her life direction. She had made an appointment to get a special kind of clairvoyant reading from Cayce—what he called a "life reading" because it would describe the patterns of her soul and the deepest purposes for her life.

Agnes had been told that she could be present to hear the reading from Cayce, even though it was more customary for him to do his psychic work at a distance and have his secretary send a transcript of all he said from the trance state. She knew what it would take to begin to diminish her anxieties about the future. Already scribbled on a piece of paper in her purse were four questions she hoped to ask at the end of the reading:

- Where should I live in order to be of the most service?
- Toward what sort of work or endeavors should I direct my energies?
- Am I correct in feeling that I have some sort of writing talent to make use of?
- How can I discipline myself at my age to do what is mine to do?

On May 16 at four o'clock in the afternoon she got her chance. Seated comfortably in Mr. Cayce's study, she watched the most remarkable series of events in her life. With his wife, Gertrude, and his secretary, Gladys, in the room as well, Cayce took a few short moments for prayer and then lay down on a couch. As Agnes watched, it looked to her as if he was simply falling asleep to take a nap. But no sooner had he begun to drift off than Gertrude recited a hypnotic-like suggestion aloud, words that instructed Cayce's higher mind to find the records of Agnes' own soul and its intentions for this lifetime.

For the next forty-five minutes, Edgar Cayce spoke from this trance state. His pace was slow and even, and it retained much of his own Southern accent. The tone of his voice had an extraordinary authority to it, but it was mixed with compassion for her and a sensitivity to the struggles that she now faced. Her key talents and skills were described. Then her weaknesses and faults were gently portrayed. And then near the end of this psychic reading, her special gift was outlined—the most creative kind of service that she could undertake to be helpful to others. This mission of her soul involved the publication of books and articles that would be useful and uplifting to men, women, and children. Her role, however, was not to be an author but rather an editor—one whose good judgment in selection and skills in reshaping words could make an invaluable contribution.

Finally, Cayce announced that he was ready for any questions. This was her opportunity. Opening the folded piece of paper in her hand, she read to him the first question: "Where should I locate myself for my best service?" Cayce's response was Washington, D.C., because for the remainder of her lifetime it would be "the center of the world," figuratively speaking. (3003-1)

Next she asked, "Along what lines should I turn my energies and interest?" Cayce's answer went back to his previous recommendations and advocated the publishing field.

These references to the world of publishing hadn't come as a surprise to her because she had already felt a pull in that direction. In fact, the third question she had prepared in advance read, "Do I have any ability in the writing field?" To this third inquiry, Cayce went into detail describing his vision of where her real talent lay. He clarified the role of editor, guide, and reviewer of the creative writing of others. It was to that kind of service that her soul was called.

Then came her final question. This was the subject that troubled her most. Even with all this good advice from Cayce, she wondered if would she be able to discipline herself, put aside her worries and doubts, and *actually do* what her soul longed to do? In response to this deep concern, Cayce offered his prescription. It was to start each day in the right way. She was instructed to repeat three times and then listen: "Lord, what would thou have me do today?" Cayce warned her against making this an empty routine. She had to mean it *and* believe that an answer would always come.

Apparently this prescription began to work for Agnes in the weeks that followed. She wrote to Cayce two months later, telling him how much his reading had meant to her. She was actively working on her meditative attunement with God. As she put it in her letter, Cayce's advice and prescriptions had "added zest to living and living aright!"

Although this advice was given more than fifty years ago, it's as applicable to us today as it was to this one woman to whom Cayce spoke. Our troubles, worries, or stresses may be somewhat different than hers, but there is a universal quality to this positive habit recommended by Cayce. This next story is an example.

A Modern Day Success with This Positive Habit

Alan is a middle level manager for a medium size company. He's also a father of two children, and his wife has a full time job. Like so many families their lives are full and busy. There are ample opportunities to get caught up in the big and little stresses that arise daily at home and at work.

"Starting the day right" has become a regular discipline for Alan since he first read about this suggestion from Cayce. It's become a positive habit that gets his life off on the right foot each morning. On those rare occasions when he forgets to make optimal use of the first minute upon awakening, he usually pays the price before the morning is half over. Here, in his own words, are his reflections and thoughts from one week of putting this creative pattern to work:

"Morning has come to be a very special time for me. Of course, there are some mornings when I don't particularly want to get up and be about the day. But as I've practiced Cayce's prescription for right use of the first minute of the day, I've discovered how I can set a wonderful tone for everything that will follow."

Alan usually awakened rather gradually, and didn't seem to need an alarm clock—making it easier for him to try this positive habit. "And when that moment comes in the early morning when I know I'm now awake and that the day will soon be starting for me, I turn my mind to the best use of my first minute. Because there's frequently the tendency in me to drift back into the hypnagogic state or even back into sleep, I've found a way stabilize my clear, wakeful consciousness. I simply focus all my attention on my breathing, usually for three rounds of inhalation and exhalation. I make those breaths slow, full, and deep. It probably takes me about thirty or forty seconds."

By that point he was ready to turn his attention to Cayce's specific recommendation. In order to connect with his individuality, visualization was the technique that worked best for him. "First, I simply say silently within myself the phrase 'my individuality' or 'my best self.' The words are really an invitation to my inner self to come forth. It's an invitation to remember a time in my past when I was deeply in touch with that individuality self. Having said silently the invitation phrase, I try to keep very still and let a memory surface. When it comes, I visualize it for about ten or fifteen seconds, as clearly and vividly as I possibly can that morning. I try to re-create the situation or scene in my imagination, and for that moment I let myself become the person I was back then." And when this process was working well for Alan, he would actually experience the emotional flavor of what was going on inside himself in the event or circumstance.

Certain memories seem to come up frequently. For example, here's one memory that he described as coming up several times. "It happened more than ten years ago. I had gone on a business trip to San Diego and I was staying at the home of friends. I arrived in the early afternoon, but the work I'd come for wasn't until the next day. My friends had picked me up at the airport and taken me home to the suburb La Jolla, where I had the remainder of the day at leisure. After getting settled into the guest bedroom, I decided to take a walk through the residential neighborhood and enjoy the beauty of this warm February day. As I started the walk, I had lots of problems on my mind. There were worries about things from the office. What's more, this was also a rather lonely time in my life, and I would easily slip into feeling sorry for myself.

"But as I continued on this walk—which eventually lasted for at least an hour—something began to change. It was as if all that stuff of personality began to melt away. I was shedding those worries and self-doubts. All those familiar stresses gradually disappeared for about thirty minutes. What came forth was a very centered and very peaceful me. I was in no hurry to finish the walk. There was no particular destination that I was straining toward, no goal to which I was compulsively fixated. Instead, I was simply walking mindfully and in touch with my feelings and my surroundings. What seemed particularly striking about this remarkable sense of myself was this realization: *that very identity was always nearby*, it was always right at hand even though my stresses and worries usually blocked it out."

That experience of his individuality self was extraordinarily vivid. And whenever it came back to mind in his first waking minute of the morning, he could easily recreate in his imagination just the way he felt that day. He could visualize the scene and could reconnect with that part of himself for fifteen or twenty seconds while lying there in bed.

"Once I've used a memory of my individuality—the meditative walk or any other memory that arises that day—then I turn my attention to an inner question, just as Cayce prescribed. I ask, 'God, what would You have me do today?' I usually pose the question about three times, staying attentive and silent for about ten seconds each time. I try to listen for a prompting, an urge, or an intuitive feeling about something that should be a priority for that day. Sometimes what comes to mind is not so much a specific job to be accomplished but instead a particular quality that it's my task to live fully that day. It might be joyfulness or appreciation or persistence. On other occasions the inspiration that comes to me in that first minute of the day is the name or face of someone I know. It's as if I'm being reminded that there is something very important for me to do in relationship to that person today. Rarely do I know immediately what that something is. My job is to pay attention to that person carefully enough that I can sense his or her needs and be responsive."

But there were many mornings when he posed the inner question; and as he tried to listen, *nothing* came. It was tempting on those mornings to feel like he had failed, but he had to remind himself of the deeper purpose to this one minute positive habit described by Cayce. The real goal was to get in touch with a certain openness to being guided and shown the way. Even if the message or the guidance didn't come in that first minute, he still had gotten in touch with his willingness to be directed. If he could trust that the direction *would* come, then often it did in the first few hours of day.

He reported one typical episode. "A good example of this process happened to me this week. Monday morning I followed the Cayce prescription for how to start the day, but at the end of that minute, no particular guidance came to me. I knew I had made a good connection with the part of me that is *willing* to be guided. However, at that point, no direction came forth. An hour and a half later I was on my way to work, ready for what was sure to be a very busy and demanding week of work. Within the first thirty minutes of being at the office, I received my guidance. It became very obvious what God wanted me to do that day.

"The message came as an event, a sort of synchronistic occurrence. I was surprised to suddenly confront in the hallway a fellow employee with whom I'd been having lots of trouble lately. He works in another building of our company's complex, and I almost never see him in the building where I work. My surprise at seeing him was *quickly* replaced by an inner knowing: working through my resentments and frustrations with him was the number one priority for the day. I found it natural and easy to say to him, 'When you're finished with what you're doing, can you come up to my office for a few minutes?'

"Ten minutes later we were alone together. What followed during the next half hour was a healing experience for both of us. There were tense moments as we talked about recent situations in which we had misunderstood each other's motives. One thing especially helped me during those times: I remembered my early morning one minute positive habit. I'd take one slow centering breath, try to remember my own best self *and his*, and then try to make as reconciling a response as I could. In the end he left to go back to his office, and I'm sure that we both felt that our relationship was now better than it had ever been before. And I'm just as sure that none of this could have turned out so well without that creative habit for starting my day right."

Applying This Positive Habit to Your Life

Make a commitment for one week to start the day right. Each morning of the test period, upon first awakening, dedicate the first minute or two to this positive habit. You may find it helpful to get yourself fully awake by focusing all your attention initially on about three slow, deep breaths. Then invite a memory of your individuality self to surface. Silently say the words "my best self" or "individuality self" and be still for a moment until a specific memory comes to mind. When one does, take about fifteen seconds to vividly recall the situation or event. Reexperience how it feels to be that part of yourself.

Finally pose the request for guidance. Use whatever version of these words works best for you: God, what would You have me do this day? Then be inwardly alert for an inspiration or intuition. It may come as a reminder of a certain person, suggesting that this relationship is a priority for your day. The guidance might come as a feeling about the importance of a certain task or as the need for a certain quality to be expressed often during the day.

If nothing specific comes, that's OK, too. What's important is having made a connection with your individuality self and having affirmed your willingness to receive direction. As you stay mindful and attentive, the direction is likely to come soon.

MEDITATION

northsoutheastwestnorthsoutheastwestnorthsoutheast

positive energy flow

peacefu

Positive
Habit
#2

Three-Minute Meditation

Meditation has long been a tool of spiritually centered people. It offers a connection to a higher power, and it awakens a calming, harmonizing influence. Contrary to some beliefs, meditation does not take years of practice and discipline to achieve results. Nor does it require long periods of uninterrupted time. The positive habit of a regular meditation session may be more within our reach than many people have thought.

For most, the biggest obstacle is just finding the time to do it. It can be difficult when we are busy to squeeze in yet another activity. Or, even when we have had some success with a regular practice, some crisis or unexpected demand can quickly have us shifting priorities, and suddenly the steady meditation discipline is lost. Or, sometimes the obstacle is merely fatigue. When we are tired from a long day, spiritual practices are sometimes the first thing to be cut out of the evening's schedule.

The start to a remedy for all these problems is to redefine what we are expecting of ourselves and expecting from the meditation period itself. Perhaps a more modest and simplistic set of expectation will allow us to keep the positive habit going. It is important to make that inward, meditative connection, even if it is just for a short amount of time daily.

If you're already a regular meditator, or even an occasional one, you know the calming, centering impact of this spiritual discipline. But the idea of very short meditation sessions may push some of your alarm buttons. You might find yourself protesting that there are no shortcuts to inner growth. In a world of fast foods and convenience stores, surely spiritual development won't succumb to modern impatience, too! Didn't Edgar Cayce frequently prescribe *patience* and continually emphasize that it was only by slow, steady effort that one progresses to higher states of consciousness?

Patience is crucial, but the idea of making spiritual connections in as brief a time as three minutes doesn't necessarily imply shortcuts. The path to enlightenment takes years of dedication, and there are no tricks. However, the idea of condensing your meditation time is based on a basic concept—simply that living in a hectic world doesn't mean you have to give up your meditation life. Positive effects can be achieved from relatively brief times of focused silence—perhaps *much* briefer than you would have anticipated.

Cayce's suggestions to some people about the positive habit of meditation indicate that maybe *as little as three minutes* is all the investment of time you have to make, at least to keep the momentum going each day. Some day— maybe *many* days—you might find it possible to have those fifteen- or thirty-minute meditation periods, the timeframe that many people have discovered is necessary to make the deepest kind of inner connection. And if you have already found a way to set aside those more lengthy periods daily for meditation, then you'll want to keep up that invaluable discipline. These mini-meditations are *not* meant to replace the more lengthy ones. But for you, an *additional* three-minute meditation—strategically timed for a moment in your hectic day when you need to disengage from the stress—can work wonders. In fact, one research study done with several hundred meditators—experienced and inexperienced—reached an important conclusion. The researchers discovered that those who got the best results from Cayce's recommendation for miniature meditation periods were the people who *already* had going a regular meditation discipline of fifteen to thirty minutes daily. The novice meditators had significant success, too; but not as dramatic as those who were already experienced meditators.

Consider just how reasonable it really is to find those three minutes daily for this crucial recentering habit. Aren't there frequent instances daily when you waste three minutes or spend that amount of time superficially—reading a mindless article, watching a little more television than is necessary, complaining about how you were mistreated earlier in the day. What happens if you remember that you have an option for how to spend that time and creative energy? As an alternative, you can find a spot to yourself, close your eyes and quiet down, and then make a connection to your more authentic self.

It boils down to developing the habit to take three minutes out of a hectic or confusing day and to refocus on what's best within you. Maybe that means taking three minutes before breakfast; or perhaps, three minutes in the middle of the afternoon. In fact, it doesn't even need to be at the same time each day. Find the time that is best for you each day. For some people the tip off that it's time for such a mini-meditation is when they begin to feel the high stress of what's going on around them. The need becomes acute for a spiritual refresher. Other people have found that the most can be gained once the day is nearly done and they have had time to unwind.

If you feel ready to give this positive habit a try, don't become too consumed with the mechanics. For example, don't become obsessed with whether or not you log precisely three minutes. It may be two or three or four—whatever feels spirit-led that day. The point is to realize that you can make a connection to your spiritual source in a relatively short amount of time. What's important is that you give it a try and that you attempt to build it into your lifestyle as a positive habit.

THE MEANING AND PURPOSE OF MEDITATION

Meditation is listening to the divine within. It is like an oasis of peace in the midst of hectic schedules and worrisome responsibilities. In those few minutes of daily quiet, it's possible to keep yourself centered and tranquil. You can connect directly with a higher consciousness that lives within you, and that momentary connection can have effects that last all day long.

But anyone who has tried to keep a regular meditation discipline knows that it doesn't always work quite as well as expected. There are days when you may get up from your meditation session and feel no more peaceful than you did when you sat down. What's gone wrong on days like that?

The trouble is most likely a misunderstanding about the very purpose of meditation. The fault may lie with our attitude about what we're trying to accomplish. If you carry into meditation the familiar mind-set of daily living, then the results from your meditation will probably be frustrating. Consider what happens when you try to transplant into your meditation period the competitive, acquisitive approach that usually characterizes modern life. It doesn't work.

What is it about this familiar approach to life that makes it so ill-suited for meditation? Throughout most of our waking hours we're striving—even straining—to reach goals and accomplish tasks. We're attempting to acquire things, such as physical possessions or people's approval.

Often our efforts are tinged with competition as we try to prove ourselves. Simply put, we're trying to *get* something.

But what happens if you attempt to carry that approach with you into meditation? For example, what's bound to occur if you try "to get peace" through meditation the same way you try to earn the boss's approval at work or complete a trip to the grocery store in less than an hour? It backfires. That straining, acquisitive attitude is the very opposite of authentic meditation. At this point you've lost touch with the real purpose of meditation. Without realizing it, your meditation life can turn into an extension of your daily life. It's a subtle thing, but that's probably the reason many people go through dry spells in which meditation just doesn't seem to work for them anymore.

Watch what can happen if "relieving stress" or "acquiring peace" has become the goal of meditation just like all the other goals of material life. You sit down for your quiet time and you already have in mind what you want: peace of mind. It's now become a commodity, just like a loaf of bread from the store or a larger return on your stock investment. It's something you want, and now you're going to use a technique to get it. Concentrating very hard on a series of words or a symbol, you go on the hunt. You're stalking peace. It's hiding somewhere in the fortress of your inner mind. And you imagine that the power of your concentration will track it down. Starting off such a meditation period, you feel sure that within a few minutes peace will belong to you. But sad to say, after a while, you'll find yourself getting up from your meditation spot in frustration or dissatisfaction because you're no closer to peace.

So, what *will* work? What's the right understanding of purpose that can relieve stress and bring peace of mind? The key is simple: *giving* rather than getting. It's a matter of surrendering yourself. First surrendering your worries. Being willing to give up your expectations, and not ex-

pecting to get anything—not even peace. The whole purpose of this meditation session is to *give*.

Sitting down for your quiet period—whether it's to be
three minutes or thirty—you choose a symbol or, better
yet, a few words that capture the essence of your own highest value in life—what Cayce called a spiritual ideal. When
you use a few carefully chosen words for your focal point,
Cayce referred to it as an "affirmation." The role of those
words is simply to help you open your feelings to something bigger than yourself. You're not out to get something;
instead, you're offering yourself to God. "Here I am. I give
up . . . my fears . . . my worries. I surrender . . . my agenda
. . . my sense of what's needed."

That basic purpose of turning oneself over to the Creator is the heart of genuine meditation. Such a foundation
comes before any technique or method. That fundamental
sense of what you do as you meditate is beyond a clever
maneuver in consciousness. It is simply a heartfelt offering of oneself to something Bigger. It is a gift of yourself
to whatever you hold as your spiritual ideal.

And then, remarkably, what comes *as a byproduct* is the
relief of stress and the experience of real peace of mind.
What a strange paradox. It's only when you're willing to
give up the goal of acquiring peace that the gift of peace is
presented to you. That is the basic spiritual mystery of
meditation.

THE ELEMENTS OF A THREE-MINUTE MEDITATION

Minute #1. These brief periods for spiritual attunement
can best be accomplished by dedicating about one minute
to each of three distinct phases. The first element is attention to your breathing. Cayce was certainly not the first to
recommend the usefulness of the breath for evoking a shift
in consciousness. It is an ancient tradition worldwide.
Some meditation techniques, for example, use attentive-

ness to the breath as the central method for focusing the mind.

Probably more than any other bodily function, the breath represents life itself. As you draw each breath into your lungs, you are revitalized. As you exhale the air, you are cleansed. This great rhythm is a symbol in your body of all the cycles of nature. No wonder that so many meditation teachers suggest that by silently focusing on your own breathing you can begin to connect to higher states of consciousness.

One way to get started with this powerful meditation tool is to simply observe your own breath for a minute. You might even count silently each breath for about sixty seconds. For most people this means about ten breath cycles. If you use this approach, don't worry about manipulating your rate or depth of inhalation. Simply relax and let your body find its own pace. Your goal is to experience the process of breathing as consciously as possible.

A slightly different approach was recommended in the Cayce readings. It was a specific breathing exercise adapted from Yoga technique. It, too, takes about a minute to complete. Cover the left nostril. Inhale through the right and exhale through the mouth. Do this three times. Next, cover the right nostril and breathe in through the left, followed by an exhale through the right nostril only. Repeat this a second and a third time. As you do this one-minute breath exercise, try to let all your thoughts be identifying with your breathing.

Minute #2. The second element of the three-minute meditation is the core of the practice—silent focus upon an affirmation. In meditations of more traditional length, this part would take fifteen, twenty, or more minutes. But in these mini-meditation sessions it will be shortened to just sixty seconds.

An affirmation, which plays a key role in the meditation technique, is a short verbal expression of a spiritual ideal.

It could be as brief as one word or as long as a full sentence. Some meditators like to compose their own spiritual phrases, others pick a phrase out of the Bible or a favorite prayer. Pick an affirmation that has personal appeal and meaning in your life. Is there a quality that you especially strive for now in your life, such as patience, joy, or faith? Write down a prayerful phrase or sentence that affirms that quality.

An affirmation is a tool that helps you, the meditator, get in touch with or "attune yourself to" your real spiritual identity. Focusing attention on your affirmation is a method for becoming sensitive to what the Cayce readings call your "individuality self" or "higher self." An affirmation that is deeply personal to you is one that will evoke positive emotions, insights, and experiences. Say the affirmation silently or aloud once or twice. Then, be receptive. Remember that it's said that prayer is "talking to God," while "meditation is listening to the Divine within." You won't necessarily hear an audible voice. More likely you'll receive a feeling or inspiration that reminds you of the truth contained in the words of your affirmation.

Don't be discouraged if your attention drifts after just ten or fifteen seconds, especially if meditation is new for you. Simply restate your affirmation in your mind and focus your thoughts again. Don't force your attention on your affirmation; rather, gently guide it.

Minute #3. The Cayce readings recommend that any meditation session, however long or short, should end with prayer for healing. That's the third phase of the meditation—in this case, just another one-minute period to send blessings to those for whom you have concern and for yourself. Remember that healing prayer doesn't limit itself to prayer for those who are physically ill. It encompasses emotional, attitudinal, and spiritual issues as well. Send a positive thought or blessing to just a few individuals for whom you may have some concern. If a person hasn't directly asked you for prayer, it's best not to visualize some specific changes happening in his or her life. It works best to surround the person mentally with the loving energy that has been awakened from this meditation session.

A Story from the Cayce Archives

Marcus lived in New Bern, North Carolina, with his wife and two-year-old son. He had been to Virginia Beach a few times, and he had visited the Cayce family at their home near the oceanfront. Marcus was interested in having a life reading from Mr. Cayce, but the waiting list was lengthy and he had a considerable delay. In February 1931, as the time for his reading drew nearer, he wrote to Cayce about his expectations.

"I am anxiously looking forward to the time when you will be able to get to my life reading, as it is a matter of vital interest to me. My affairs have reached the point where it is time for me to make some sort of change but I will hold off until I hear from you as I feel that this reading is to be the turning point in my life."

Marcus was a healthy man overall; but the inevitable stress of his career combined with approaching middle age wore at his health in subtle ways. He wanted to find out how to live a more balanced life, giving his body the attention it needed in order to remain healthy for the long run.

In April of 1931, the appointment date for his reading arrived. Gertrude Cayce presided over the session, as Edgar Cayce offered his wisdom from a deep, unconscious state. First Cayce addressed the minor health concerns that Marcus had expressed. With his clairvoyant insight, Cayce indicated that Marcus' left eye would improve over time, and that his poor digestion would be improved by drinking a glass of warm water upon waking up each morning.

When he had been preparing questions for this reading

months earlier, Marcus knew the tremendous amount of stress he felt each day was his most immediate health problem. He had worded one of his questions for the reading, "How can I overcome the nerve strain I'm under at times?"

The answer from Cayce on this day in April was direct and simple. "By closing the eyes and meditating from within, so that there arises—through that of the nerve system—that necessary elements . . . that will quiet the whole nerve forces, making for that—as has been given—as the *true* bread, the true strength of life itself. Quiet, meditation, for a half to a minute, will bring strength—will the body see *physically* this flowing out to quiet self, whether walking, standing still, or resting. Well, too, that *oft* when alone *meditate* in the silence—as the body *has* done." (311-4)

This extraordinary recommendation—for quiet meditation lasting perhaps only half a minute or one minute—contained a powerful promise. By developing the positive habit of recentering himself each day with mini-meditation sessions, he could heal this nervous tension disorder.

The reading helped Marcus get his health back on track and gave him personal insights into the mind-body connection. Profoundly impressed with the information Cayce gave him, Marcus wrote to Cayce a few months later:

"As time goes on the original life reading gets clearer and the meaning more apparent to me. I wish everyone who has had a life reading would get it out about every three months and carefully check up on the statements made and the events as they unfold. It is a revelation."

A Modern Day Success with This Positive Habit

Most mornings when Ron headed to work, he felt like he was headed into a war zone. Things were tough at his company, a large telecommunications business with thousands of employees overall and more than seven hundred at the facility where he worked as human resources manager. The company was in flux, having just purchased and merged with another firm, and there was considerable pressure on Ron and his team to effect many personnel changes. Staying centered had become an elusive feature in his life.

If things at home had been a little more stable, it might have been easier for Ron to stay connected to his inner resources. It wasn't that anything was particularly wrong with his family life, but everything there seemed to be in the midst of change, too. His wife had just started a new job and there were the expected stresses of adapting to a different set of work colleagues and duties. One of their children was just off to college, and both parents felt a continuing obligation to stay in touch with him and be supportive as he learned a new lifestyle away from home. And their thirteen-year-old daughter was showing some normal but occasionally annoying behavior of a new teenager.

After a particularly rough day at work—one that involved breaking the news to five employees that their jobs would soon be phased out—he came home in need of a little refuge and rejuvenation. Driving home he had thought about resources available to him to keep his life on track, especially during this challenging transition time at the office, which was sure to last at least two more months. One option seemed to be a recommitment to daily meditation. It was something he had learned and even practiced regularly when he was in his twenties, but for the last ten years or so he had been very sporadic with the discipline. As he pulled into his driveway that evening, his enthusiasm for the idea of regular meditation had grown to the point that he wanted to have his first session right away.

However, as soon as he walked into house he realized that it wasn't going to happen soon. His daughter announced that Ron's boss had called ten minutes earlier and needed a call back as soon as possible. What's more his daughter needed a ride to a friend's house in half an hour, and with his wife having to work late at her new job, Ron would have to be the chauffeur.

The interrupted plan repeated the same pattern each day for the rest of the week, and before long Ron realized that he had to come up with a new approach. By a fortunate and serendipitous event, he came across an article about meditation that mentioned the way in which positive benefits could come from even brief periods of focused attention. The idea was a novelty to him because he had always imagined that it took at least thirty minutes to have a meaningful meditation session. But given the demands of his life at the time, this concept of miniature meditation times seemed too good to pass up.

He started the new habit that very day, first with a three-minute meditation just before dinnertime. He wasn't sure that much came from that initial try, largely because he spent most of the three minutes mentally fighting off self-doubts that he could really do it right. Ron persisted, though. He experimented with different times of day to try his mini-meditation. Mornings on the one hand seemed easiest to get himself centered and focused in a short amount of time. But the very best results came from the time and place that he would have least expected to be successful—right there at his office.

Ron had never considered doing a spiritual practice like meditation in his office. It would be embarrassing if someone walked in on him sitting in his chair with eyes closed and no evidence that he was doing anything productive. What's more, everything about his office had associations for him that are linked to stresses in his life: His telephone that is constantly ringing with people's problems, his computer on which he frequently works and reworks salary budgets, stacks of personnel files with employees' performance appraisals. This was hardly a "sacred space" for him.

Surprisingly, however, he was quickly able to establish a powerful daily habit of three-minute meditations in the early afternoon. He shed his anxiety about someone discovering him in the midst of a meditation period. There was an easy and truthful answer should that situation ever arise. He was taking time for some creative thinking. The feared interruption by another employee never took place, and within a week of regular practice he had discovered a dramatic change in how the rest of his day would unfold.

Of course, there were still the issues and problems that beset any human resources manager of a company in transition. If anything, the difficulties and challenges actually got a little worse soon after he started the positive habit of mini-meditations. The dramatic change for him personally was the ability to stay calm and clearheaded in the midst of it all. Something about those short, meditative moments would reconnect him with the best within himself.

When an employee came into his office with angry, demanding words, Ron found it considerably easier to be tolerant and patient. When his boss required yet another reworking of the budget, Ron felt himself a little more quickly able to accept the task graciously. Of course, there were instances when the stresses got to him, and he became frustrated or discouraged. The three-minute meditations didn't make him a saint. But something was now different, and that "something" was clearly the result of this new positive habit.

APPLYING THIS POSITIVE HABIT TO YOUR LIFE

If you don't already have a regular meditation discipline, this is the chance to get a positive habit started with short periods each day. If, on the other hand, you already have a steady pattern of regular meditation sessions, then keep that in place while you add three-minute meditations daily as a supplement.

Try different times of day and different situations to experiment with these mini-meditations. Perhaps early in the morning, if you are somewhat rushed to get out of the house, you could still find time to devote three minutes to this activity. Or, maybe midmorning at work when everyone else is taking a coffee break. Perhaps you'll get good results by having a short meditation in the very late afternoon before starting to get ready for the evening meal and the remainder of the day. Just play with various possibilities and see what works best for you.

As you practice three-minute meditation sessions, keep in mind that what really counts isn't quantity but quality. Those few moments, sincerely and enthusiastically approached, can be just as powerful as any more lengthy devotional time. Let yourself experience how, in the timelessness of your soul life, spiritual centering can take place whenever you have a mind and a will for it.

PRACTICING SELF-OBSERVATION

Positive
Habit
#3

The Inner Witness: Practicing
Self-Observation

The person who is living a spiritually centered life has the
sense of two sides of the self and has found a creative way
to coordinate them. These two aspects can be called the
personality and the individuality, and the positive habit of
loving, objective self-observation is the key to how they
best relate to each other.

The purpose of self-observation is to remember our best
selves, our true selves. In the effort to put our best selves at
the forefront, we must filter through the debris of our automatic, unconscious habits, the traits that keep us stuck in
life. Through the self-observation process we step back and
see the personality, with all its positive and negative facets, and ultimately come to the core of our being—our individuality. The individuality is one's ideal personified.

Let's consider more carefully these two sides to
everyone's being, a topic introduced in the first chapter.
Personality is the outside shell, that which we show to most
of the world, not because it is the best indication of who
we are, but simply by routine. In fact, mechanical routines
of attitude, emotion, and action are what make up our personality, the patterns we have gathered from infancy from
whoever and whatever have been influencing factors in
our lives. The compilation of gathered characteristics re-

sembles a tree in form. Like large branches that sprout off to small branches that, in turn, sprout off leaves, each trait builds and depends on another. And so, we may often find in the process of self-observation that we start seeing the connections between our thoughts, feelings, and behaviors—especially those that operate by strong negative patterns and make life unproductive.

When we operate solely from the direction of our personalities, without understanding of our individualities, trouble lies ahead. When personality rules, we are captured by automatic patterns and are unable to break free of negative or less desirable traits. Even though letting the personality govern our actions might feel familiar or comfortable, we are blocking ourselves from what our deepest and best self has the potential to achieve.

Individuality, though usually less familiar to us, is the more genuine form of ourselves, and it is not a product of outside influences. It is the identity of our spirit, and a healthy spiritual life requires guidance from that individuality.

All of this is not so say, however, that the personality is always "bad" and the individuality is the only source of "good." Rather, the individuality is a more authentic expression of who we really are ourselves, as opposed to worn-out or diminished expressions of what others expect us to value, believe in, or do.

THE WITNESSING SELF

Observation is one of the most simple, automatic activities of our daily lives. We are observing all the time, sometimes consciously, sometimes without realizing it. It is easy to observe situations that involve other people, but how easy is it to observe ourselves?

Self-observation is fairly easily done on a superficial level. We can stand in front of the mirror and decide if our shoes really complement our blouse; we can listen to a tape recording of our public presentation and decide if the closing statement really drove home the point. But this kind of self-observation is tainted with biases and judgments from which we have difficulty letting go. They easily cloud the self-observation process.

To be an objective observer of self is challenging. After all, to be "objective" usually means not to be "involved" in the situation, and who is more involved in our lives than we ourselves? But objective self-observation is far from impossible; it just takes close attention and steady practice.

It is a technique that was described by Cayce with the recommendation to "stand aside and watch self go by." Other philosophers and psychologists have referred to the identical process, but with different labels. The technique sounds a little tricky, though. We may wonder, "How can I watch myself? I *am* myself."

The key to understanding the workings of this technique is to see the many roles we play in our personality, the different "selves" that we have. In our daily lives most of us portray dozens of sides of our personality: the parent, the friend, the boss, the colleague, or the customer. Each role we play is ruled by the habits formed in our personality. "Standing aside and watching yourself go by" involves the observation of these "selves" we play each day.

Self-observation involves the development of an extra focus of attention, a new kind of consciousness. With one part of our attention we continue to be consumed by our personality and its reactions to the events and situations in which we are involved. But then we split our attention and let the second half become "the witnessing self." It is as if a part of us steps out of our life and simply watches. This witnessing self is acutely conscious of the feelings, thoughts, and actions of daily life. We stand apart from ourselves and look back at our personality.

It is important to remember that the witnessing self is part of the personality and not the individuality. We are not standing back and letting one part of ourselves be critiqued by the higher self. Instead, the witnessing self is simply another "self" played by the personality, no more special or significant than another. So it must refrain from the temptation to judge.

Consider the following example of self-observation. For several years a man kept the positive habit of reviewing just before falling asleep his activities from the day now ending. Then he learns about the technique of standing aside and watching self go by. Already familiar with his nightly after-the-fact self-observations, he assumes this method will be easy to perform. But his well-practiced expertise lies in reviewing the day's events after, not during, their occurrence. Now he is embarking on an even more demanding discipline: to observe himself as fully as possible "in the now," as the events are happening.

The man discovers that he has trouble splitting his attention in the midst of living his life, and he struggles greatly with the new discipline. In all kinds of situations he attempts to be aware of his behavior routines and his automatic mind dialogues. But the attention of a "witnessing self" is constantly interrupted by other trains of thought.

One afternoon, after weeks of struggling to "split" his attention by means of self-observation, he becomes angry with a gas attendant who will not allow credit card payment at the pump. A sign says it's allowed, and the man doesn't want the inconvenience of having to walk all the way over to the teller. They exchange harsh words across the station pavement, and the man leaves in a huff. Extremely mad and frustrated, the man is caught up in a flurry of angry dialogue in his head. As he drives away, he notices his gas cap bouncing down the road after him because he had removed it at the pump and absentmindedly put it on top of the car before the argument.

But the silly sight in the rearview mirror of his gas cap getting hopelessly lost in the traffic behind him suddenly awakened something in him—that witnessing identity. The witnessing self separated with its attention, and it now started observing the mental dialogue. It could immediately see how the "angry customer" side of his personality had been dealing with the situation in an almost unconscious knee-jerk, reactive way. The man was able to hold the witnessing attention only for a minute, and then it vanished. But in that time, he stepped out of the situation and observed how he handled it. The witnessing self gave him the perspective to see that the situation didn't necessarily demand rage.

This kind of self-observation is a powerful, positive habit for spiritually centered people. Once there has been some initial success with this method, it can lead to more than just recognizing specific traits or aspects of the personality. Self-observation applied to our lives lets us recognize the *patterns* and *themes* that seemingly control us and keep us from fulfilling our potential.

For example, a woman was in an unhappy relationship with her boyfriend. She was reluctant to end the relationship because she feared that he was the best she would find. But the problems were too great to ignore and she dumped him.

Dating again, the woman saw that she had nothing to fear; there were plenty of nice men to choose from. After a short time she found herself involved with a wonderful man, and everything was going as well as it could. But soon she began to be disillusioned with him; the same issues arose with the new man as with the previous boyfriend. Convinced that all the men she meets are the same horrible package, she ended the second relationship.

But the problem is not the boyfriends; the problem is the woman. The state of her inner being—her level of consciousness—is identical in dealing with both men. She is perpetuating the unproductive theme in which she finds herself. Nothing had changed from the first man to the second; it was a different boyfriend but she is in the same relationship.

In a similar fashion, by practicing the positive habit of self-observation, you may find yourself recognizing recurrent themes. You may see a pattern in your past and present that keeps being relived. And when you identify such themes, you'll likely find that the outcome of these repeated patterns doesn't make you very happy.

A Story from the Cayce Archives

Surely the best examples of self-observation come from the spiritual development group to whom Cayce first uttered the advice to "stand aside and watch self go by." This collection of men and women from diverse walks of life shared an interest in the 1930s in Cayce's healing and spiritual growth work. Some of them even aspired to awaken intuitive gifts of their own.

On a weekly basis for more than a decade, this group of about fifteen met with Cayce to discuss progress on applying spiritual teachings that he had presented to them. A specific growth sequence was proposed—a sort of spiritual development curriculum—and the individual group members were challenged to put the ideas into practical application.

One of the early lessons in this sequence called the "A Search for God" material concerned the need for deeper self-knowledge. Of course, this is an ancient idea, as evidenced by the famous injunction of the Delphic oracle to "know thyself." In readings given to the group specifically about the awakening of great self-knowledge, Cayce recommended that they learn to practice "standing aside and watching self go by."

The statement was first made to a woman in her forties who was a devoted member of the group. In a question-and-answer exchange with Cayce, Helena asked how she could come to know herself more deeply, even as she was known by her Creator. Cayce replied, "Being able to, as it were, *literally,* stand aside and watch self pass by! Take the time to occasionally be sufficiently introspective of that, that may happen in self's relation to others, to *see* the reactions of others as to that as was done by self; for true—as it has been said—no man lives to himself, no man dies to himself; for as the currents run to bring about the forces that are so necessary to man's own in these material things, so are those forces in self active upon those whom we act upon. Being able, then, to see self as others see you; for, as has been given, '*Now* we know in part, then shall we know even as we are known.'" (262-9)

In the months and years that followed, Helena and the other members of the group continually tried to practice self-observation, even as they moved on to other lessons in the growth sequence. Some two years later, she received advice from Cayce directly about her own life challenges, many of them daunting issues related to her family and career. She was having problems in her work as a book-keeper, in large part because of the inclination of her boss to lose his temper. But Cayce advised greater self-awareness as part of the antidote. She had an automatic emotional reaction of being hurt, and he suggested that with more self-awareness she could stay spiritually centered in this trying circumstance. "Then, let not that which has been said so hurt self as to cause self to act, say or do that which would not be in keeping with the policy, the activity, the life of self in the relationships that have existed . . . " (303-4)

Even more difficult were the problems at home. Again, the advice she had gotten two years earlier about self-observation would serve her well. In regard to unharmonious relations with her twenty-two-year-old daughter, Cayce pushed her to see the patterns *in herself* that were largely contributing to the problems. "For, as conditions exist, self lies in the way . . . " It was no doubt hard for Helena to have to admit that she herself was at the center of the problem. And just as tough for us can be the task of getting to know, through self-observation, the many patterns of our own personalities.

A MODERN DAY SUCCESS WITH THIS POSITIVE HABIT

One springtime Rita got involved helping her husband John shoot some video footage to promote his upcoming book, about which the couple was very excited. Although talented in their respective careers, neither of them had any experience making a professional quality video, and so it was frustrating work. Rita operated the rented video camera, with difficulty, while John stood in front of it speaking.

"Mechanical things frequently baffle me. When I can't figure out how to work an appliance, like a sewing machine, computer, or camera, I fall into a mind trap of thinking that I must figure it out for myself, even if someone is there who could help if I asked. The more I insist on doing it myself, the more frustrated, angry, and stupid I feel."

The initial videotaping session ended in a fever of frustration. They didn't have a finished product worthy of being shown, and it was apparent that a better version wasn't going to manifest itself that afternoon. They gave up for the day. As they were putting away the equipment, Rita began to feel very emotional. "I detected a fleeting moment of sorrow, not noticeable to John, and barely noticeable to me."

Though mildly felt in that instance, the feeling of failure was a familiar one. Rita went to the bedroom to record in her journal the negative emotions brought on by the frustration of the videotaping session. As she wrote, she began to cry. She flipped through the pages of her journal and saw that the halfway point had almost been reached. It was pages and pages of recorded emotions of failure, worthlessness, and sorrow—accounts of emotions similar to those that motivated her writing now. It was not the camera itself, nor in the past had it been any of the other simple situations that brought on such intense feelings of failure. Rather, it was something inside herself, something that dictated such hurtful feelings by force of habit. Sitting on her bed with her journal in hand, Rita reflected on the past year's writings.

"Now overwhelmed by emotion, I saw that my life had been a lie to the extent that when good things had happened to other people, even those close to me, in the midst of celebration, this touch of sorrow had always surfaced . . . not jealousy. I realized that all my years in the Search for God study groups had been for naught because it had never touched or healed this miserable part of myself. I was devoured by feelings of humiliation, valuelessness, and unworthiness . . . then panic as I realized that no one must ever know about this. If they did, no one would ever share their successes or believe I was truly glad for them. My mind was numb and I felt sick when the emotions finally subsided."

Rita began to observe herself closely and intensely in hopes of discovering her self-destructive tendencies and of making progress healing them. Her first step was to admit that she had a problem. That gave her a sense of relief because to a problem, of course, there is a solution. Rita's journal served as her outlet for her emotions, her record of her self-observation. She recorded her emotions all the time instead of only when she felt out of control. She spent time remembering the times that she had felt the worst, and contemplated what might have triggered it.

In her mind, Rita relived the video camera episode, trying to identify at what point she lost control of her emotions. Her careful scrutiny of the problem left her with a bit of assurance that the videotapes could be attempted again and completed.

"I was trying to reassure and encourage John, and to my shock found I was telling him exactly what had happened to me (emotionally). He made a joke, not realizing the intensity of my emotions that I was probably covering over, and I began to cry uncontrollably." But it was a blessing in disguise. "As traumatic as crying was, I value it immensely for the gift of self-awareness and healing it brought."

Rita came face to face with her self-destructive tendencies and her awareness was increased. The healing process was jump-started as she began to see how her inattention to her own needs had led to guilt and feelings of inadequacy.

"I have problems with spending money. I have a hard time buying something just for me, even when I need it. I apologize over purchases, then try to justify them. This does not extend to household needs or other family members, only to me."

It was as if Rita didn't feel she deserved anything new or to be taken care of in general. She decided that her gross neglect of herself had extended to almost every part of her life, especially her career.

"My basic misconception was that I will never have real accomplishment in my life because I am unworthy, flawed, stupid, and not deserving of success. When something good happens to me, I often don't feel happy. For example, a photo that I submitted to a regional magazine was used in a layout. Instead of feeling elated, I declared I wasn't 'really' a good photographer because technically I didn't know very much about taking pictures. This attitude also prevails when I am complimented. Instead of appreciating and expressing thankfulness, I devalue myself and internally remind myself of all my failures, thinking, if they 'really' knew me, they'd know my success was an accident."

Identifying the problem through loving, objective self-observation was a major step and within a month of discovering her basic misperception of herself, Rita had made significant progress in correcting the problem. Whenever she felt herself reverting to negative self-talk, she would remind herself of one good quality she possessed. Also, reminding herself of simple facts was a key. For example, operating a video camera is difficult, and no one should expect professional results on her first try. Her frustrating first try did not make her stupid. Perhaps those who were skilled with a video camera couldn't cook or play as good a golf game as she could. And by remembering the positive, Rita began to combat the situations that produced her tears.

"I am working on identifying when to ask for help sooner. I am trying to lighten up by remembering that mistakes are just part of being alive and usually not fatal. I am trying to remember to claim and appreciate all the good that is in my life, and simply say, 'Thank you.'"

It was through gaining a greater picture of herself, both her negative traits and her positive attributes, that Rita began to heal from a lifetime of self-destructive attitudes. Rita had gained a new perspective on life through observing the worst parts of her personality and actively combating them.

"So often in the past, I have compared my accomplishments with what others have done and mine seem so paltry, useless and uninspired. And when I think of all the people in the world, I have felt lost in a sea of nothingness. But an image of a fingerprint has often flitted through my mind as I worked on myself. When I think of the fingerprint, and how each person has their own unique pattern, I see that I too was created as an original with my own mark to add to the beauty of the whole—not better than, but just as necessary as those I admire. My self-observation is soul work that has the potential to last me my lifetime."

APPLYING THIS POSITIVE HABIT TO YOUR LIFE

Try to practice self-observation, even for just a minute at a time, but at least three times daily. At first this may sound like it's too easy a target, but you are likely to discover that some days it's difficult to accomplish even this modest goal. Our involvement with ruts, routines, and patterns is very strong. Try though to observe:

- Your "inner talk," the internal dialogue between parts of your personality;
- Your emotions that surface automatically in response to situations that arise;
- Your behaviors and actions that seem to happen almost like being on automatic pilot.

As you have these moments of intentional witnessing, guard against any impulse to judge or criticize. Ironically, at the moment you've stepped aside with part of your attention, there is a strong tendency to place a value judgment on what you've observed. But as soon as you've become critical or prideful, you've actually lost the inner separation of self-observation, you've re-identified with it, and you've come back under its spell.

Witnessing consciousness can therefore be understood as moments of dis-identifying with aspects of the routine, mechanical personality. Just that momentary separation is the beginning of freedom from the pattern or routine! Being able to stand aside and watch the pattern must mean that there is *some* part of you that is *not* that pattern. And that momentary realization can be the start of remembering that you have a deeper and more authentic self—your individuality.

*Positive
Habit
#4*

The Pace of Life

Of all the fables and stories we learned as children, perhaps none applies better to modern life than the story of
the tortoise and the hare. In the fable, the hare ran quickly
in an effort to win the race but, because of his speed, became tired and lost the race to the slow steadily moving
turtle. In the end, quickness loses out to steady stamina.

Most of us are a combination of qualities from the tortoise and the hare. We can easily become caught in a wild
swing between extremes. We hurry up, only to have to en-
dure waiting. We rush around frantically and then collapse
in exhaustion.

Perhaps you've noticed, though, that your highest quality efforts in life come from a place that integrate those
two extremes. It has the lively enthusiasm and energy of
the hare, but it also has the steady commitment of the tortoise. When you are dealing with something you really care
about, you tend to find a pacing and timing that drifts to
neither extreme. It's at that point of balance—where we
reach the ideal pace of life—that our best selves can come
through revealing a more creative, sensitive, and skilled
side of our personalities. In fact, the skill for finding a pace
of life that reflects balance is one of the positive habits
of spiritually centered people. Let's look a little more

closely at how they do it.

Think about your life in terms of the two opposite poles. Perhaps one extreme in you thinks that the best way to accomplish something is a driven, urgent frame of mind. It says, "Calm, relaxed days are nice, but realistically, if I want to get something done, then I've got to shift into high gear." But even if that is the way we are most efficient, at what price to our overall health and well-being do things get accomplished? A supercharged life can throw us so badly off our equilibrium that quickly the quality of living suffers drastically. Too easily it can leave us stressed out and tense, compromising both our physical and spiritual health.

At the same time, a life that is too laid-back and relaxed may not be healthy either. If we lack any sense of timing, urgency, or importance to what we do, we will be as bad off as those who try to hurry to get too much done in a short amount of time.

How do you find your ideal pace of life? It can start with beginning to watch yourself a little more closely. Observe yourself during the day and become more sensitive to feelings of hurriedness or of laziness. Does life feel slow paced—so much so, perhaps, that you have succumbed to feelings of inertia, idleness, or fatigue? Or, on the other hand, does your life feel rushed and tense, maybe with the sense that you'll never get done all the things you've expected of yourself that day? Of course, the observations you make may vary from day to day, even from hour to hour. However, for most of us, there are strong patterns. We tend to have slipped into one extreme or the other.

Now think about what would be an optimal pace for your life. What would allow you to be relaxed and peaceful but at the same time eager to get things done with right timing. Consider choosing a "target pace," one that is either slightly more mellow *or* slightly more urgent than your current routine. Then work a little each day to meet your target, to adjust yourself to the kind of optimal pacing that characterizes spiritually centered people. Let's see how this might work, first for those people who need to set a "faster" target pace.

Problem #1: Picking Up the Pace

Some days it simply seems too hard to get going. Maybe low energy or lack of motivation is to blame. Sometimes it's just hard to get into the swing of things; there isn't really any incentive or inspiration. What's going on? Can this feeling be remedied?

Lots of people came to Cayce searching for answers to issues like these. For some it had become a slowdown of life to the point of desperation. In his counsel, Cayce emphasized that neither stress nor idleness was optimal. A balance was required—one that could provide motivation *and* sufficient time for reflection and relaxation. He gave general guidelines for how to go about capturing that elusive equilibrium.

Of course, first is the need to consider the possibility of a medical condition that needs the attention of a physician—hopefully a doctor who appreciates the connections of body, mind, and spirit. Severely diminished energy or motivation might denote depression or chronic fatigue. But even in the situations that may need medication, Cayce's additional advice about attitudinal and behavior changes can be part of the overall prescription for health and happiness. Here are some of those non-medical suggestions.

Look for Possibilities. A teenage girl asked in her reading from Cayce, "How can I keep from giving the impression that I'm asleep or indolent?" (5256-1) Cayce answered, "Awaken to the possibilities within." That response points out an important fact—monotony leads to lack of motivation, while variety and options make life stimulating. Choices usually do not just fall into our laps;

life does not just happen to us. We need to search out possibilities and find them, instead of relying on fate to provide us with an interesting assortment of experiences. When we are actively creating possibilities, life gets exciting again.

Look at your own life in that light. Where do you have options and possibilities? Even if you feel stuck in certain areas of your life, there may be a variety of ways in which you can inwardly meet those challenges. There are endless possibilities wrapped up in how you deal with a situation, even if you can't necessarily change the situation right away. But you can create options that start with your attitudes. For example, you might not be able to stop your boss from having a negative demeanor, but you have all the control over how you deal with him or her. Or, you might have the potentially boring duty to pick the kids up from school every day, but you can still choose to go a different route each day or take them on a little adventure occasionally as you head home. Life is full of possibilities that you can control.

As another arena for exploring possibilities, think about your various talents and interests. Which would you like to explore more fully? We have the blessing to live at a time in history when people are freer to explore options and possibilities than ever before. Never before have there been so many options for how to use our talents and interests. Be creative; take some risks and explore things that are new to you. Go to a play; take a walk in nature; read the biography of someone who has inspired you.

Get Your Body Moving. When a thirty-six-year-old man asked Cayce what would make his life more harmonious, he received the following advice, "Do not let [life] become a drudge or a drag. Be exercised or interested . . . " (315-9)

It's amazing to see how potent a little bit of physical activity can be, especially when it's fun. That's why Cayce added the qualifier "be interested." An exercise program done routinely and with begrudging effort won't have balancing effects. But even a brief period of physical activity that matches your interests can have a powerfully revitalizing impact. Study after study finds that people that exercise regularly have more energy and lead happier, healthier lives. Exercise has numerous mental benefits. One study even found that regular exercise and antidepressants were equally effective in the treatment of depression. So find a sport or activity that is fun for you; and, if you don't already have a favorite, try a new one.

Make Decisions. Sometimes the pace of life lags because we've been avoiding the use of free will. We may have been trying to sidestep a major decision, or maybe we just put off minor decision-making because we don't have the motivation to do it. One woman asked Cayce, "Is what is holding me back physical or laziness?" (922-1) In other words, she wondered if her inertia was due to a health problem or to a character shortcoming. The answer she received put the emphasis on her free will without trying to pinpoint either of the two alternatives she had imagined. "Rather that of indecision . . . " was Cayce's analysis.

When you feel stuck and the pace of your life has slowed to a crawl, ask yourself what decisions you need to make to speed it up once again. What needs to change? See if you can identify choice points that you have been avoiding. Perhaps your life can't get on properly until you make up your mind and use your will.

Have a Single Priority. This sort of advice came from Cayce in a variety of ways. One thirty-year-old woman was told that her life of drudgery was linked to an unclaimed vision. The woman, who called herself indecisive, asked in her reading, "Why do I not make a more continuous effort?" In response, Cayce asked rhetorically, "Is thy purpose a single one?" (922-1)

The point here is oneness of intention. Does your life have a primary priority? Do you have a central ideal that is guiding you? If, instead, you have a muddle of competing purposes, then it's easy to see how gridlock can set it. The remedy is simply to do a little self-analysis and hone in on the vision of your life that you want to direct more purposefully. Clarifying that point can get you going again.

Problem #2: Slowing Down the Pace

For many people, the modern world presents a continual challenge to stay centered and not get carried away by hectic lifestyles. Life sometimes goes by faster than we are able to catch up. Constantly living an over-scheduled life can lead to mental and physical fatigue. In order to function smoothly and efficiently we need to find a pace of life that is healthy—one that allows for rest time while tending to our responsibilities, as well. Here are some keys for doing just that.

Be Patient with Yourself. How much of your strain is coming from self-criticism? Are you pushing yourself to achieve more than can be expected realistically? Have you set a deadline that is virtually impossible to reach? When you have too much to do, you can often lose your perspective. And when you get caught in the cycle of self-criticism, every little fault or shortcoming becomes a magnified hurdle to your success.

Keep things in perspective. People's shortcomings are generally not intentional. This is not to say that responsibility for mistakes should be erased. But nothing is gained by wasting energy on frustration. Be patient, and this includes showing self-patience just as you would show it to others. Be kind and tolerant to yourself. Leave space in your planning for your mistakes *and* other people's, as well. Of course, this advice doesn't mean to expect yourself or others to fall short; but, when little, unplanned problems arrive, they will be less consequential if you stay flexible. In summary, if you are the kind of person who is easily frustrated, show yourself patience first, then it will be easier to be patient with others.

"Make Haste Slowly." This curious proverb is found time and time again in Cayce's recommendations for a more centered life. Although the phrase seems to be an oxymoron, there is wisdom in these seemingly contradictory words.

Think of the words in a context broader than the familiar usage. Usually haste is equated with hurrying and rushing. But that is only the narrow meaning of the word. *Haste* has another meaning as well: efficiency of action, doing things the right way. This interpretation is expressed in an old and nowadays infrequently quoted adage, "The more haste, the less speed." In other words, in your commitment to let your best self come through, you must first find the speed or pace that will allow you to be *most efficient.* Sometimes that requires a fast tempo, but more often than not it means going more slowly.

"Make haste slowly." Keep committed to how important it is to do your best. Hold onto your desires and ideals; practice steady efforts. Perhaps you will find that it's possible to move through life at a calm, deliberate pace while keeping an inner sense of urgency and priority. What you are striving for in life *is* important, so important that it's worth moving slowly, if need be, in order to have efficiency and success.

Don't Get Ahead of Yourself. Strain is one of the worst results of a fast-paced life. It's a matter of trying to stretch beyond the present moment and beyond what is possible for right now. Many of us with busy lives can recall a familiar feeling—a disenchantment that so much needs to get done that nothing ends up being done very well. If you stretch yourself too thin, your performance will suffer. Athletes and performers refer to this phenomenon. They do their best only by "staying within themselves." If they stretch themselves too far, they lose control of their movements and their performance suffers.

Keep a Positive Attitude About Tension. Tension is one of the villains of the modern age, producing a wide range of mental and physical ailments. There is no medicine for tension, no magic cure. Rather its origin and solution lie in the way we deal with demanding situations and the way we manage our time. Tension impairs our good judgment and our sense of balance. When we react out of the tension, almost invariably the situation is made only worse.

Where does that tension come from? There are certainly times when it arises from needless worry or paralyzing fear. But that's not always the case, and one useful tool for finding the right pace of life can start with your very attitude toward tension itself. Occasionally, you may notice a type of tension that comes from energetic vitality—an excitement about doing certain activities, even though perhaps you are doing them too fast or there are too many of them at once. When this is the case, back off a bit. Appreciate how wonderful it is to have such enthusiasm for the opportunities all around you! Then, find a way to enjoy the chance to be doing so many interesting things but without rushing though life. That was the advice Cayce gave one person.

A nineteen-year-old woman wrote to Cayce to find out why she felt such tension and what could be done about it. "Why am I so tense?" she asked in her reading. Cayce responded, "For you are so alive! . . . Tenseness here, for this entity, bespeaks the vitality, the desire to be *doing*." (2403-1)

A Story from the Cayce Archives

Helen worked in the publishing field in New York City during the Depression Era. She had recently remarried, and she and her new husband were raising her son from the previous marriage. Her new husband was a writer and also interested in psychical research. He had learned of Edgar

Cayce's work through some of these psychic studies and had referred several friends to Cayce for readings. In the summer of 1935, all three members of the family obtained personal readings for guidance and life purpose.

Helen felt great pressure to be successful and provide for her fifteen-year-old son. In a letter to Cayce, she reflected on the tensions in her life and the way in which daily responsibilities had made it very hard to recover from some of her health problems. "Certain nerve exhausting difficulties—jammed subway travel, personal difficulties with the office and editorial workers under my jurisdiction, etc., etc. have *retarded* my recovery I am sure . . . Being the bread winner of the family (with a son to be educated somehow) for the present, have made it impossible for me to give my health problems *first* attention. I have had to fight the battle on *all fronts at once* and the same time—it seems to me. I have pleaded with 'the powers that be' to help me, and though discouraged, am not giving up the battle, but still struggling along as best I know how." Her words, no doubt, strike a note of familiarity for many of us living in our own hectic situations that seem to force a pace of life that pushes spiritual and health priorities aside.

In a reading for her that summer, Cayce first gave a comprehensive picture of Helen's temperament and approach to life. He identified her natural skills for leadership, initiative, and power; but he went on to warn her that too frequently she looked to others for promptings about when and how to use these skills. You too frequently slip into being a dependent leader rather than an independent one, he observed. Then he went on to describe her vulnerability to be "'taken in' by sympathies of others," and her difficulty in knowing when to demand answers for the things happening in her life. "The entity oft is in the position of not questioning when it should and questioning when it shouldn't." (967-1)

Cayce addressed the issue of life's pace most directly in response to Helen's query about how she could speed up desired result in her career. Cayce tried to shift her point of view on the matter of tempo to her progress. The good that she was doing in her job needed to have a chance to be absorbed by those touched through her work. She wasn't allowing time for her good efforts to materialize so that, in turn, she could build on them. Any impatience would, in effect, tend to get her ahead of herself. As Cayce put it, "The results as attained, the service as rendered, must be that to enable the entity to make haste slowly. Do not get ahead of the *good* that is rendered, else we will find the same confusions arising oft."

Cayce's advice to Helen is sound advice for any of us today who are looking for spiritually centered and productive lives. Cayce would say, even to us, "Pace yourself. Keep in mind how nice it is to reap the benefits of your hard work, to see how well you are doing. Finding a right tempo will allow you to build on the foundation of yesterday's accomplishments."

A MODERN DAY SUCCESS WITH THIS POSITIVE HABIT

In a world where most people think that "finding the right pace to life" means slowing down, it's interesting to see examples in which a spark to *enliven* the pace of life is needed.

Mary Ellen taught second grade at public school. It was her ninth year at the elementary school, and she still had great enthusiasm for her work. "I *love* kids. I love all their different personalities, and how they interact with each other. They keep it simple and sweet, sometimes messy and mean, but they are just being themselves. I think adults can learn a lot from being around kids. My job is fun, not only do I get to hang out with my favorite age group all day long, I get to teach them to read, write, and do math. It is the most satisfying feeling to help a child sound out a word and then hear him read the sentence and look so pleased with himself."

Another reason Mary Ellen loved her job was that it allowed her to spend the afternoons with her two children. She was a single mother with a seven-year-old girl and a ten-year-old boy. Her two kids kept her busy. During the school year her life was an array of soccer practice, ballet classes, slumber parties, and birthday parties. By dinnertime, Mary Ellen had usually carted kids around in the blue minivan from one end of their suburban stomping grounds to the other. After dinner there was homework to be done and lesson plans to create for her second graders.

Overall Mary Ellen loved her life; it was comfortable and fulfilling most of the year. During the school year, she and the children had found a happy, balanced pace for living. But the last few summers had been a different story. As a teacher, she had nearly three months off from work. Thinking that she really needed the extra money, she had tried unsuccessfully for several consecutive years to obtain a summer school position. But those jobs always filled up quickly, and she hadn't been able to get one.

A second factor made Mary Ellen's summers so different from the rest of the year. Her son and daughter always went to visit their father in Pennsylvania for the better part of summer vacation. So, Mary Ellen was left without a job to occupy her time and without her children to keep her company. It was lonely without her kids, but it did offer her time for herself, something that was a rare luxury during the school year.

"I had gotten in to the habit of taking a nice vacation with some of my girlfriends—also teachers—with summer weeks to spare. One year we went to the Bahamas, another to Mexico. For the most recent summer, these friends were planning a large-scale trip to Costa Rica to trek in the rainforests. Money had been a little tight that spring, so I decided to skip the trip."

With most of Mary Ellen's good friends gone, her kids visiting their father, and no summer school job to occupy her time, she was seemingly left with nothing to do. At first, she was excited. She would sleep well into the morning, sometimes even until noon. She would make breakfast and sit on the porch under a big umbrella. She read three novels in two weeks.

But after a few weeks, her idleness wasn't much fun anymore. She found herself sleeping when she didn't have anything else to do. She had fallen into such an all-encompassing pattern of taking-it-easy that she never had the desire to go out at night or look for stimulating activities during the day.

"I felt incredibly useless. I think I was becoming depressed."

Usually a bubbly, fun-loving person, Mary Ellen found herself less excited, less humorous. Her energy was at an all-time low, and she had become so used to sleeping that she required ten hours per night. Her pace of life had not just slowed down; it was virtually at a standstill. She recognized the problem but wasn't sure how to find a solution.

The feelings of fatigue and boredom had been going on for almost a month when, by chance, Mary Ellen ran into a family friend, Catherine, at the supermarket on a Saturday morning. Catherine had her three children with her and was rolling a shopping cart brimming with groceries. The kids were running up and down the aisles pestering the shoppers. Mary Ellen recognized Catherine immediately and went over to say hello. The two had a nice chat about their children and their jobs. Catherine was still working full time in the marketing department of a major department store. The job was fun, she got a chance to be creative, and she had received two promotions since the two women had talked last.

"It was almost instinctive that I asked Catherine what she did with her kids during the summer. I usually don't get into that with parents since my kids spend the summers in Pittsburgh. I guess I could just sense Catherine's desperation."

Catherine didn't have a place to send her kids on Monday. The babysitter, with whom she had only been moderately satisfied, had given two days notice before going on vacation for two weeks. Catherine had been so flustered upon hearing the babysitter's announcement that she had exchanged harsh words with the woman. Now she would be too embarrassed to ask the babysitter for her continued services. So, for the coming week, Catherine told Mary Ellen there in the supermarket, she supposed that she would just have to depend on the grandparents, although they lived an hour's drive away. This would be only a short-term solution, and she would have to find something closer.

Mary Ellen came up with an idea. Why didn't *she* watch the kids for a week until Catherine could set up something permanent? Catherine couldn't impose, but Mary Ellen could see the excitement in Catherine's face. No, she really wouldn't mind at all, she loved kids.

"Bethany, Michael, and Josh began coming to my home at 8:00 a.m. My house is perfect for kids. The backyard is enormous, and there are both swings and a sandbox. The neighbors are a retired couple with a swimming pool. My family and guests have always been welcome to use it, so I took Catherine's kids over a couple of times. We had a delightful time together."

A week went by, then two. Catherine didn't mention any other childcare, and Mary Ellen didn't ask. Finally, Mary Ellen formally offered to take care of the three children for the rest of the summer. She was beginning to really enjoy it, and Catherine looked relieved. She said she had put in some requests for childcare but nothing could top Mary Ellen. The kids just loved her.

Mary Ellen began to think about possibilities related to these babysitting sessions. Why limit it to Catherine's kids? She could provide her friends with a safe, fun place for their children during the summer workdays, and at the same time she could supplement her income. Mary Ellen pulled out her Rolodex. She put in calls to a few friends and acquaintances with small children. Three days later, Mary Ellen had a class of ten children, ranging from five to eleven years old. She took on a neighborhood high school girl for added supervision. The group planned trips to the beach, the aquarium, and the park. For those summer mornings, Mary Ellen was excited once again just to be waking up and having an adventure ahead. Her days were full of what she loved, and she spent the summer happily.

"I have only done the daytime playgroup for one summer, but it was a big hit. Every parent wants us to continue. Next summer we are thinking about renting out some space and having a couple of other teachers join in, too. We want to continue something this special."

Applying This Positive Habit to Your Life

Try a one-week experiment in which you'll try to carefully monitor the pace of your day. You'll have a goal—a "target pace"—that you'll pick. And as much as possible you'll try to keep in sync with that tempo for your day. When you catch yourself going to one extreme or the other, you'll try to bring it back to your target.

For this application experiment, we'll use a playful analogy: driving your car at a certain speed. This will simply be an imaginative, symbolic way that we can talk about the tempo of your life as you're experiencing it. (It does *not* have to do with the literal speed you'll be driving your automobile during the week!) For example, at what "speed" does it feel like your life is going recently? Are you constantly racing from one thing to another? Then, maybe you'd say your life is going seventy-five mph. Or, perhaps your life has become boring and almost stagnant. In that case, maybe you'd say it feels like ten mph. If you keep a journal or diary, you might even want to make note of this average pace number as you start your experimental week. (Of course, that pace has probably varied; but overall, what's been the average?) It may not have been the ideal pace, but honestly make note of what it has been.

Next, think about what would be the *ideal* pace for you. Pick a number, still using the automobile speed analogy. What's a good balance point which you suspect would allow the best in you to come out? That number will symbolize your "target pace" for the week's experiment. Make a written note of that ideal number, too.

Now, for the coming week, make a special effort to pace your life optimally. When you start to get too rushed, slow down. Maybe one of the four approaches outlined in this chapter will help. Or, if you get too bogged down, try to pick up the tempo to match your "target pace." Again, one of the methods suggested earlier in this chapter may be just the prescription for you.

Positive
Habit
#5

Balanced Living

Balance in life. It's one of the simplest concepts for healthy living, but it's also one of the most difficult to find. There's so much that threatens to pull us to one extreme or another. It's so easy to overdo it—when it comes to eating, investing time and energy, or relating to other people. There are so many ways to go to one extreme or another, to let events throw you off kilter. Most of us have lives filled with countless factors to juggle and demands to meet. It can be quite overwhelming.

In order to have a healthy lifestyle—physically, mentally, and spiritually—we must be *artists of balance* in every respect. By finding balance in just one area of life, we can feel more in control of life as a whole.

Even before times were as hurried and scattered as our own, Edgar Cayce frequently counseled people about the necessity to stay balanced. In fact, it's one of the central principles in his teachings, found in virtually every different type of reading. For example, a key to health is described as equilibrium among the many back-and-forth interactions of the body, such as assimilation and elimination. And recommendations for a healthy lifestyle included balance between work and recreation. As one reading put it: "All work and no play is as bad as all play with no work." (2597-2)

In other types of readings, the same theme was emphasized. Dreams were sometimes interpreted by Cayce as experiences of the soul that come to balance us from extremes we may have exhibited in waking life. As one reading said: "Oft [dreams] may be as opposite that which is presented to the body . . . " (1968-10) In a similar way, the secret of loving, vital human relations is to learn balanced ways of interaction—mutual levels of support and care.

In fact, balance is such a crucial principle, according to Cayce, that without it we're unlikely to fulfill the purpose for which we were born. In rather dramatic terms, one thirty-eight-year-old man was told in his reading, "And unless . . . the experience [is] well-balanced, the entity *cannot, will* not fulfill the purpose for which it came into the present experience." (1537-1)

If balance is potentially so important, how can we go about investigating its impact? There are probably as many points where we could test balance as there are aspects of our lives. But creating balance in life is not achieved by rigid control over our activities. Don't let the little voice inside you *demand* balance. If you try to force balance on yourself, it will become just another time-consuming demand, like housework or errands.

Instead, use a more gradual approach. Start by playfully exploring how balance might operate in just *one or two* specific parts of your life. Concentrate on those areas without being distracted by others. Choosing just two areas is more realistic than a complete overhaul of your life.

In this chapter we'll focus on how you can start creating a positive habit of balance in two particular arenas: one concerning diet and another related to relationships. Creating habits of balance is a process. The goal is to have the positive habits become routine, automatic, and naturally part of your life. In both these areas of life, we'll find that "balance" doesn't necessarily mean 50-50. Instead, it means "right ratio," the proper amount of each element in order to make things work best.

ALKALINE/ACID FOOD BALANCE

Although there are many specific recommendations from Cayce regarding advisable and inadvisable foods, perhaps the most significant dietary suggestion concerns a type of balance between two categories of food and how they metabolize in your body. To understand how Cayce classified foods, we need to recognize that digestion and metabolism are chemical processes. If you eat something, such as a piece of bread, your body breaks down its components to make use of its energy and nutrients. The chemical process leaves a residue, a chemical remainder that is either alkaline or acidic in nature.

So, in grouping foods as alkaline or acidic, we don't distinguish on the basis of the food itself but instead on how it reacts in the body. Sometimes this classification can be puzzling. For example, citrus fruit is obviously acidic in itself, but when it's metabolized in the body it leaves an alkaline residue. Therefore, a grapefruit is categorized as alkaline-producing.

Alkaline-producing	Acid-producing
All fruits (fresh and dried) except prunes, plums, cranberries	All dairy products
	Refined sugars
	All meats, including seafood
All vegetables (except legumes such as peas, beans, lentils) and rhubarb	Egg whites
	Legumes (peas, beans, lentils)
	Nuts and peanuts
	All other high protein foods
	Prunes, plums, cranberries
	All cereals/grains, including breads, cakes
	Animal fats, including fish oils

The Cayce readings encourage us to try for a diet that is made up of 80 percent alkaline-producing foods and 20 percent acid-producing. For many of us, this is no easy task. Our dietary habits may be far from this goal. Take a look at the preceding chart that describes the most common elements of our diet.

So why does the body need such a high percentage of alkaline-producing foods? They keep the metabolism steady by entering the bloodstream at constant levels, whereas acid-producers throw the metabolism off balance. According to Cayce's health philosophy, alkaline-producing foods have specific benefits such as the ability to aid the repair of cells. He stated that green leafy vegetables help to purify the blood and ward off infection, while celery and carrots help to strengthen the nerves. All the health benefits of keeping the optimal acid/ alkaline ratio should encourage us to start developing some better habits of nutrition.

Think about your diet in terms of the 80:20 ratio. Probably most of us have some work to do. Don't be discouraged if your diet is closer to the opposite ratio. The farther from the goal you are, the more dramatic improvements in health you can potentially experience. But there are likely to be obstacles to improvement. It can be difficult to have balance in a diet when you frequently eat "on the go," but not impossible. You may find that friends and family members aren't very supportive of your interest in developing new diet habits. But the biggest obstacle can be your own unconsciousness of what you are doing everyday. So, start creating balance by *increasing your awareness* of what you are eating. It may even be helpful to record your eating habits initially.

After observing your diet for a few days, set a realistic goal for improvement. If a typical day's diet is 30 percent alkaline and 70 percent acid, try for a 50:50 ratio. That, in itself, will stretch you, and it may produce some significant changes. Or, if you're already at 50:50, then you might be ready to discipline yourself and try for the optimum suggested by Cayce.

One reason for setting a realistic goal is to make success more likely. But there are other reasons, too. If you share meals with family members, even though there's probably room for some individual differences, you are going to need to take into consideration their needs and expectations in a meal. Another reason is that changes in the diet probably should not be too dramatic. To go from 20/80 percent to 80/20 percent overnight might more likely produce upsetting effects in the body than promote health. Be gradual and be realistic. Changes in your diet take discipline and effort.

BALANCING RELATIONSHIPS

Food balancing—even if it's hard to achieve—is straightforward and directly measurable. When it comes to keeping relationships balanced, the matter becomes a little more elusive. First we have to decide which relationships to focus on. Many of us have so many demands from so many people, that it would appear to be a hopeless task to try keep them all balanced.

But an interesting solution presents itself from the examples of spiritually centered people. We can look for balance in this part of our lives especially in terms of two categories: the relationships one has with *others*, and the relationship one has with *self*. In other words, a place where we most easily get out of balance concerns the relative amount of time and energy spent nurturing a healthy relationship with ourselves.

This concept was featured in Cayce's advice given to a sixty-six-year-old woman. Her purpose in initially contacting him was to get suggestions for curing her morning headaches. After that first reading, she asked for a life reading in which broader recommendations for health and balance were offered. One piece of advice to her was something that we can all test in our own lives: "For he that contributes only to his own welfare soon finds little to work for. He that contributes only to the welfare of others soon finds too much of others and has lost the appreciation of self, or of its ideals." (3478-2) What a remarkable call to balance!

If we recall the passage quoted earlier that links soul purpose to balance, then the advice to this woman—and to us *all*—suggests that fulfilling her mission in life requires a healthy equilibrium in relations with others *and* her relationship with self. In other words, it's possible to go through "burnout" in which so much is focused on the needs of others that one loses "the appreciation of self."

On another occasion, Cayce told a twenty-eight-year-old man to recognize the two sides of the mission for which each and every soul incarnates: serving God *and* appreciating oneself. The reading put it this way: " . . . ye are to fulfill the purpose for which each soul enters the earth—which is to manifest to the glory of God and to the honor of self." (3333-1) In other words, genuine love of oneself—which is quite different from selfishness, which ignores the needs of others—has a very important role to play in a balanced, healthy life. We should find time to invest in ourselves. Activities that nurture the best within us are not only valid and useful, they're indispensable. It's the positive habit of balance in its most potent expression.

So, how good of a job are you doing with this kind of balance? Remember that "balance" doesn't necessarily mean 50-50. We're looking instead for "right ratio," that which allows the best in life to come forth.

Take inventory of your time. How balanced have you recently been in regard to contributing to the welfare of others versus contributing to the welfare of yourself? Perhaps you need to make it a priority to spend some time each day alone, whether that means practicing spiritual disciplines, painting your toenails, or reading a non-work-related book. Unlike the alkaline-acid balance, there is no magic number to be spent on self-nurturance compared to time spent with others. Some days you might only have ten minutes; other days you might have a few hours. Weave the positive habit of balance into the relationships you have with other people and with yourself.

A STORY FROM THE CAYCE ARCHIVES

David is a good example of the kind of person who developed a long-standing spiritual guidance relationship with Edgar Cayce and turned to him for advice on a wide variety of issues. From 1935 through 1942 he consulted with Cayce on an average of once per year, usually when something very important was happening in his life.

The initial contact came because of David's positive habit for getting exercise at a New York City gym, one that was affiliated with Cayce's friend Dr. Harold Reilly. Because of Reilly's openness to Cayce's natural medicine approach, many recipients of Cayce's health recommendations had found their way to Dr. Reilly for treatment. As a thirty-one-year-old interested in physical fitness, David came to the health club and gym just for a regular tune-up. Then, one day he was injured in the boxing ring, and Dr. Reilly wasn't able to come up with a treatment that seemed to work. Following Reilly suggestion, an inquiry letter was sent to Cayce for advice.

In the letter, David explained his problem this way. "My physical trouble is in my left shoulder and extends down the arm and fingers of that side. It may be neuritis. Many months ago while boxing at Reilly's gym I shot out a crooked punch or 'round hook' which caused me a slight bit of pain; so that perhaps I have a torn ligament in that region, in which a cold has settled. The index and two fingers of my left hand are rendered senseless while the entire arm, shoulder and back near the neck are in constant pain. It reacts to nothing that Reilly has been able to do, so far. I had it x-rayed, but no bone fractures show up . . . "

Following the advice in that first reading led to David becoming more intrigued with this unusual man in Virginia. As the years passed, he consulted Cayce on issues ranging from the need for a tonsillectomy to marriage prospects with a specific young woman to his literary projects. Although he called himself a "publicist" by trade, he felt his calling was broader. For his second reading from Cayce, his written inquiries included this question: "I have jumped back and forth between the literary and journalistic fields and the musical field. Which of these do I 'belong' in, from an astral view? And are my faculties more critical than creative? That is, ought I to prosecute my urges as a playwright (creative) or remain in the field of theatrical criticism? Or ought I to 'chuck' both and 'go popular'—'go Hollywood'—and do popular entertainment for mass consumption?"

Cayce's advice was to look for the opportunities with plays and short stories, although he implied that it might be as much *helping other writers* as it would be composing the plays or stories himself.

Nevertheless, David pursued his dream to be a playwright, and in the winter of 1942 he had begun to formulate the outline of a "dramatic comedy," as he called it, entitled "The Life of Reilly." This endeavor would ultimately lead to some valuable spiritual advice about how important it is for every one of us to find the right balance between the needs of others and our own needs.

Cayce was encouraging of the writing plans, saying that he could find collaborators in Hollywood; and if it were approached properly, it would reach many people and be very successful financially. But "it should also carry a lesson," as Cayce put it—even a tone that would help in the defense of the American way of life. (This at a time when the United States had two months earlier entered World War II.)

Ten months later David was back for another reading. The motivation was apparently twofold. Things had soured in his relationship with a woman eighteen years his junior, and he hoped that Cayce would help him understand the lessons for his soul that were contained in that disappointing break-up. *And*, he had finished the first draft of his script for the stage play, "The Life of Reilly." He wanted feedback, hoping that the moral lesson of the play would be clear. His theme was love in human relations, and he wanted his audience to learn how to best protect their own interests and needs in the midst of trying to learn how love relations work. (We cannot help but wonder how much of this play was autobiographical, given his own recently failed love affair.)

Cayce was encouraging yet corrective. "The weakness in the present script lies in that this thread is often broken, or in some portions there is the losing sight of that which is the motivating force. The humor is very good, but the approaches sometime become rough. The *idea* is good. The ideal at times is lost sight of." Then came the telling exchange as Cayce's wife Gertrude posed the key question that had been submitted by David in a letter. But she wasn't even able to finish the question before Cayce interrupted.

(Q) In the play, "The Life of Reilly," I have tried or hoped to show the evolution of personal love into that wider and more real and abiding love; to give our huge audience of the theatre and screen a glimpse of the "How to do this"—for their *own* "selfish" protection and interests.

(A) (Interrupting) That's *self*, not *selfish. Self, not selfish!* Selfish bespeaks of the devil! Self bespeaks of God! 815-7

This remarkable statement by Cayce stands at the heart of his spiritual advice to us about the place of "self" and "self-needs" in the scheme of things. "Self" is linked to our Creator. Our identity and individuality matter to God. Life requires of us the delicate balance of attending to the needs of others *and* giving sufficient attention to our own needs. Finding the right amount of time and energy to invest in ourselves is *not* wrong or selfish. Yes, there is an extreme to which we can go—one in which self-interest is all that we can understand. That's "selfishness," and it profoundly hinders spirituality. But the honoring of self is essential for anyone who wants to have a spiritually centered life. The message is as timely now as it was sixty years ago!

A MODERN DAY SUCCESS WITH THIS POSITIVE HABIT

Frank had a hectic lifestyle. His job made great demands on his time, and his health suffered because of it. Most days he picked up breakfast from the donut shop on the corner and ate it on the train to work; some days he skipped breakfast all together. Frequently his lunch was quickly eaten at his desk between phone calls. Dinner was the most balanced meal, usually because he ate out at one of his five or six favorite restaurants. Otherwise, he ate leftovers in front of the television or his laptop.

Clearly, food was a problem for Frank. He had terrible indigestion that prevented him from eating many foods and kept him from sleeping some nights. He would lie in his bed, curled up from pain. He was taking prescription antacids daily; and to make the situation worse, he drank four or five cups of coffee per day. But whenever he tried to cut back, it would mean fatigue and less efficiency in virtually every part of his life. There was simply too much he had to get done every day to be able to cut back on his beloved coffee.

"I had very bad health habits for years. My diet mainly

consisted of bread products and meat. I knew that this was not a healthy way to live, but when you are extremely busy, lifestyle changes are not always a priority. The wake-up call came for me when a man in my office had a minor heart attack. He was a smoker and like me a fan of fast food. But he was only in his late fifties. It scared me. That friend made a quick and full recovery, but the event had really shaken me. Basically it made me realize that health was important, that I had to make it a priority."

He enlisted the help of a nutritionist, and he learned from her about acid- and alkaline-reacting foods. "We went over what I ate every day. I was a little embarrassed at my child-ish eating habits, but I am sure she had seen worse."

Together, Frank and his nutritionist came up with a plan to make his dietary intake 50 percent acid-producing and 50 percent alkaline-producing. Following the plan, though, took more effort than he had expected. For example, in-stead of stopping at a fast food restaurant, he had to wake up twenty minutes earlier than normal each morning and cook himself a nutritious breakfast. He had to frequent health food stores and produce markets in order to have fresh fruits and vegetables for the alkaline side of his diet. Lunch was a little easier simply because he found a health food store with delicious lunchtime take-out salads. And he expanded his horizons for dinner, finding some new res-taurants and even cooking for himself more than he was accustomed to. The healthy foods were a challenge be-cause Frank just didn't really like the taste of vegetables, but he discovered ways to prepare them that made them tolerable.

The hardest part was changing his coffee habit. His nu-tritionist had insisted that he cut back on coffee, and ini-tially he set a goal of drinking only two cups daily instead of four or five. For the first few weeks he had difficulty staying alert in the afternoon; sometimes he would put his head down on his desk for ten minutes and snooze. But the nutritionist had promised that he would be more energetic in the long run, and slowly her prediction came true.

Frank struggled with the temptation to eat his familiar foods. But as he slowly grew to like vegetables, things became easier. It took him a month to form the positive habit of a 50:50 alkaline-acid ratio. "Just getting my diet to a 50:50 ratio helped my indigestion tremendously. Drinking fewer cups of coffee was the factor that probably made the most difference. And it's more expensive to eat well. But in the long run, it's just an investment in my health."

Four months later, Frank's diet had been transformed to a 70:30 ratio, and there were even periods where he reached the optimum of 80:20. The change beyond the 50:50 ratio had taken place not because he forced himself to do it but because he found himself wanting to eat that way. He developed a nickname among his colleagues at the office—the "health nut"—due to his complete turn around." If there is bottled water, baby carrots, or tofu in the refrigerator at work, every one knows its mine."

His doctor was impressed with his improving health. Frank was no longer dependent on the prescription pills for hyperacidity, but still took one occasionally after an unusually spicy meal. His coffee intake got down to one cup in the morning, and sometimes he even enjoyed a cup of tea instead.

Clearly his much improved health can be attributed to his new positive habits with nutrition. "Its amazing how much of a change a good diet can cause, and it is apparent how much damage a poor one makes. I don't even want to imagine the strain my body must have been under for the last ten years. Now that I have my diet in check, my general stress level is less and I have more energy. I'm going to be using that newfound energy to start making other important changes for the better." Finding balance for this one part of his life was the beginning of a self-transformation journey.

APPLYING THIS POSITIVE HABIT TO YOUR LIFE

Experiment with greater balance in your own life—remembering that "balance" means "right ratio" and that's not always 50:50. Perhaps you're willing to try changes to your alkaline-acid food balance. It might not be to the ideal Cayce recommended, but can you try a week or a month of moving the ratio in the right direction?

Or you might decide to initiate this life-changing positive habit in regard to how you invest your time and energy. What are your own self-needs, and how can you best meet them while also meeting your responsibilities to others? Here again, if it doesn't seem like you can overhaul your life right now, still look for little changes that can move you in the right direction.

Positive
Habit
#6

Self-Assertion and Healthy Will

Self-assertion and *will* seemingly have little to do with spiritual development. In the minds of some people, these two qualities actually work against soul growth. That may be true if free will is understood merely as willfulness or willpower, and if self-assertion is equated with pushiness or aggressive behavior. But a broader image of these two qualities reveals that both have an important role in the life of a spiritually centered person.

Self-assertion most basically means an affirmation of one's sense of self. It's a matter of getting in touch with the person you feel yourself to be and then projecting it outward. In this context, we assert ourselves each and every day. The actions we initiate and the responses we make to events around us are continually making statements about who we think we are. The healthy use of self-assertion is a vital positive habit for strengthening our individuality and nourishing spiritual growth.

As we think about s*elf-assertion* as *self-affirmation*, it raises the question, "*Which self* am I affirming?" We are complex human beings with many sides and facets—multiple selves. Most of us have a shallow, fear-based self within us somewhere. Through what psychologists call *projection*, we recognize it in other people more easily than in ourselves.

Most all of us have ways that we try to cover up or compensate for our fear-based self. For example, a woman with low self-esteem and a poor self-image might compensate with a cocky self-assertiveness. However, in an indirect way, that overly confident behavior really reinforces and gives energy to her fear-based self. Or, imagine a man who argues forcefully to make a point that he knows has no merit. He is probably misusing his ability to assert himself. He may actually be trying to mask the weakened position he feels.

Dealing with other people's unhealthy self-assertiveness makes human relations troubling. Encountering people like these two examples puts us to the test. If we fail to understand what is going on beneath the surface, then we're likely to get the wrong idea about self-assertion and its positive potential.

These issues are important not only to how we respond to other people's apparent self-assertiveness, they also come into focus with our own. Consider one way that the proper use of self-assertion can operate in human relations. It concerns the question of how much we firmly adhere to what we already believe, and how much we let the opinions of others shape our own thinking. It's tempting to assume that a spiritually centered person knows exactly what he or she believes and then vigorously hangs onto it— maybe even pushing a little to get others to believe the same thing.

But there is a fine line between healthy self-assertion and a closed-mindedness to the ideas of others. Totally refusing to let other people influence you is *not* a sign of a healthy psychology. What's more, pretending to know things you don't really know is a distorted form of self-assertion, and it's usually a defense mechanism. If we want to have the ability for positive self-assertion *and* we want to have good interpersonal relationships, then it's important to remember that we all have much to learn from each other. A spiritually centered person is able to consider a viewpoint that contradicts his own, consider the alternative, and make the choice of which opinion best fulfills his ideals. Then he will follow through on the choice made and abstain from second-guessing himself once the choice is made.

AFFIRMING THE BEST SELF

Understanding the use of self-assertion to affirm your best self sets the stage for the full expression of this positive habit. It's a matter of discovering in daily life how to actually assert your best self instead of your fear-based self. It starts with observing your actions each day and recognizing which part of you is shining through.

The best self is what Cayce called the *individuality*, in contrast to the more familiar identity called the *personality*. Let's consider initially this familiar side of ourselves that we usually show to the world.

The personality contains the acquired set of habit patterns with which you most often operate in life. Your personality traits have largely been learned from parents, teachers, and the culture all around you. They are made up of countless mechanical ways in which you think, feel, and act in the world. In other words, your personality is your familiar sense of identity, but it exists by habit and routine. Little or no free will is operative, and your life is more or less running on automatic pilot as you react to situations as they unfold around you. Does this sound familiar? In fact, it's a little painful and embarrassing to admit how often this is exactly the way we live.

Your personality is reactive. In an automatic and very predictable way, it responds to the events of daily life. For example, if someone says something distasteful to you, your personality responds like a machine with automatic thoughts, feelings, and behaviors. No real force of free will is involved, any more than your automobile "wills" to start its engine when you turn the ignition key. Some of the responses of your personality are "nice" and some are "not so nice." However, what all these automatic reactions have in common is their lack of conscious, willed intention. In this sense, then, each of us is "asleep" spiritually speaking when we are identified with the personality.

But as *individuality* you are a being of free will. When you are aware of and identified with individuality, you are able to make choices and be creative. Of course, your individuality is not a perfect self because it needs to grow and evolve. From the level of individuality, you are an unfolding spiritual being. This is the identity that is capable of growth, whereas your personality exists to repeat patterns and largely stay the same.

Out of your individuality self comes a balanced will. A balanced will is one that understands all the factors and opinions involved in a decision, has the ability to make a positive choice, and the courage to follow through. That's the sort of self-assertion demonstrated by spiritually centered people!

But how does one reach that healthy level of being in the world? What are the steps and methods? Even though there are no shortcuts, here are some practical ways in which you can get started toward nurturing the positive habit of using your free will to assert your best self.

Express Positive Feelings. Perhaps the expression of good feelings is not a practice that comes to mind when one thinks about self-assertion. But don't limit your picture of self-assertion to the actions that "push to get what you want" or "persuade people to see things your way."

You're probably in touch with many positive feelings each day. But how many of them do you let out? In those positive moments, try asserting yourself by expressing what you feel. Take those good feelings seriously. Speak of them. Act on them. For example, if you and your mother have a meaningful conversation that touches you deeply, let her know. "I really feel good when we can talk like this." If a co-worker does an excellent job on some task for you, thank her and let her know exactly how it makes you feel. "I just really appreciate you and how hard you worked to get this done."

Praise is an especially fruitful way to explore communicating positive feelings. For example, if your son comes home with a B on his report card in a subject that has been very tough for him, tell him that you know he worked hard and you are proud of him. "I am really pleased with what you've accomplished." Praising other people comes easily to some of us, but others have to dig deeper to find those feelings and express them. People appreciate recognition when they have worked hard, and they like to hear you assert the positive feelings it has awakened in you.

Expressing positive feelings *about yourself* is equally important, and for many people it's even more challenging than communicating positive feelings about others. We generally assume that when we have anything good to say about ourselves that we will sound prideful or "full of ourselves." Perhaps we don't tell other people how good we feel simply because we suspect those feelings might get misinterpreted and shot down, or that we might seem too egotistical. But it's as important to compliment ourselves as it is to praise others. It has to be done with delicacy and sensitivity to what others are feeling about themselves right then. There is no need to make self-assertion of positive self-feelings into any sort of comparison to other people. One can say, "Wow, I'm so pleased that I got that project done so quickly and accurately!" rather than "Boy, I did that project better and faster than anyone else in this office could have." Surprisingly, when we practice the right kind of assertion of positive self-feelings, it can even stimulate other people to start feeling the same way toward themselves.

Communicate Negative Feelings. The positive and balanced use of negative feelings is essential to self-assertion. However, it can be one of the most difficult habits to master. Rarely do people communicate negative feelings constructively. Most people have slipped into a distorted version of how this is done. They communicate negative feelings by either losing control and yelling, or by sarcasm. Or, as a form of noncommunication, they refrain from expressing the negative feelings in order to avoid conflict.

None of these options is healthy. In fact, all of these examples are misapplications of self-assertion. If we lash out with our negative feelings, we can accomplish little in the long run except making a name for ourselves as an over-reactor. If we hold it all in, the emotion festers in the unconscious and is sure to come out in an unhealthy way later. The crucial principle is simply this: *If we block or suppress negative emotions, then in the long run we subvert the positive ones as well.*

A better approach begins by identifying the behavior that has stimulated your negative feeling. Instead of blurting out, "You are rude and a sorry excuse for a friend!" try communicating more clearly, yet with no less honesty. "I am really angry that you forgot our lunch date." Or, instead of using sarcasm as a defense—"Aren't you the smartest?"—it's to your credit if you can deal with your hurt feelings more directly by saying, "I don't appreciate it when you dismiss my ideas so quickly. I worked hard on them."

A more direct approach to communicating negative feelings shouldn't strip away the emotion. There can and should be feeling in your voice. But it can be done with directness and by linking your emotion directly to a specific action that has wounded or upset you. That kind of healthy self-assertion of negative feelings maintains respect for both yourself and the other person. It's much more likely to make the exchange a productive experience.

Setting Limits. This one sounds easy and basic, but can prove to be complicated. A lot is demanded of most of us each day. Responsibilities that require attention. External demands that end up leaving little room for our own internal needs—for time, privacy, or energy. It can easily become overwhelming unless we learn to sometimes say "no" and set some limits.

We need to be able to give clear, loving, self-assertive instructions to people so they know how to treat us. If we don't learn how to set limits for what others are able to ask of us *and* what we expect of ourselves, then we're sure to get caught up in a cycle of expecting to do more than is feasible. In moments when we feel this most acutely, we need to be able to make statements like these:

- I don't want to hear critical things about other people right now.
- I have errands to run and boxes to unpack. I don't think I'm going to be able to make it to the soccer game.
- I'd love to hear what you have to say, but I have so much on my mind right now that I don't think I can give it the attention it deserves. Maybe we can talk tomorrow.

Sometimes—as with the last of these three examples—it's possible to say "yes" to something in addition to saying "no." In other words, a healthy willingness to be self-assertive by setting limits doesn't have to be exclusively negative. When you say "no" to one demand, you can also communicate what you *are* willing to do.

- I can't take your child to school this Friday, but you can check with me later about next Friday.
- I can't lend you money right now, but maybe together we can figure out some other way that I can be helpful.

Taking Initiatives. Initiatives are practical applications of principles. They are the means by which good ideas become positive habits. A healthy, self-assertive will is able to get things started, to take initiatives. When you believe in yourself—your own best self—you're likely to affirm your talents by taking initiatives. When you believe in your skills and abilities, you will want to affirm them positively each day.

This means being in touch with your needs and being willing to take charge to do whatever needs to be done to ensure that your needs are met. Usually, this requires acting. But actions often begin with words—either in the form of statements made to other people *or* affirmations that you say silently to yourself. Find yourself saying,

- I'm confident that I can do a good job if you'll give me the chance.
- I think I can help with this problem.
- I want more information about this.

Remember that the key to positive self-assertion is to know yourself—your best self—and then let that self guide your actions.

A Story from the Cayce Archives

It was early in 1943 when Herman wrote to Edgar Cayce. The letter was not unlike many Cayce received, particularly in the period just after the publication of his biography, *There Is a River*. Herman and his wife had both been deeply moved by the book and sought personal readings. Their longstanding interest in natural health methods, parapsychology, and mystical studies made them prime candidates to benefit from the advice he might have to offer.

Herman's life didn't have particular crises that were undermining his happiness. In fact he didn't feel he even had room to complain. He had a good marriage, and his work as a machinist foreman had kept him from being drafted into the army as the world war raged. But his life had slipped into a series of frustrations, particularly in regard to his career. Something was still deeply unsatisfying, and

Herman did not really know what was wrong with him. He was just unhappy, and he wrote to Cayce, "My greatest trouble seems to be not in being successful in my work or any enterprise that comes my way but in choosing a field in which I can work, help others and be a lot happier with associates than I have been thus far." (3018-1) He wanted to know what it would take for him to find happiness.

Cayce's advice to him addressed most directly the need to take control of his life. It outlined the way in which a failure of will and a lack of healthy self-assertiveness were at the root of his problem. "The entity because of his indecisions at times allows others to take advantage of him. The entity must learn to be self-assertive; not egotistical but self-assertive—from a knowledge of the relationship of self with the material world." The emphasis here was upon reinterpreting the meaning of self-assertion, of being able to see it not as egotistical pride but instead as a natural outgrowth of self-knowledge and an understanding of his relationship to the world around him. The failure to do this had allowed others to exert their own will too influentially upon him.

Cayce continued with an analysis of the need to connect with his inner power and to develop the ability to assert what Herman knew to be true. " . . . when [you] allow others to over-persuade, or when [you] rely upon others, there is not the use of the innate strength within self. It is well, to be sure, for individuals to reason together . . . but let [your] yeas be yeas and [your] nays be nays—though in the Lord . . . knowing deep within yourself you are right! Analyze the problems of the day, today, in [your] capacity as an executive officer in the machinist shop, or in whatever line of endeavor."

Herman's further questions to Cayce asked for clarification about his prospects in the future. Cayce had suggestions, even naming a particular mining company that would benefit from his talents, but the reading quickly returned to guiding principles about how he could straighten out his life. In order to become more sure of himself, he needed to deepen his faith in his Creator *and* in himself. "Who is the author, then, of [your] faith? In [yourself], in the hope of the hereafter, in the abilities of [your] mind and [your] body? He that is the way, the truth and the life!"

Cayce continued and honed in on Herman's inability to be resolute—to come to a decision and then stick to it. " . . . know [yourself] first. Know [your] own abilities. Don't assert that you know something and don't, but [you] usually *do!* Don't allow others to talk you out of decisions you have reached. This done—knowing that as [you] apply the spiritual *and* mental abilities—He will show the way, He will give the direction! . . . [You] alone may limit [yourself]. For, if the Lord is on [your] side, who may be against [you]?"

Most of us probably don't have this severe a problem with indecision and the inability to assert what we know to be true. Nevertheless, this story provides one of Cayce's most eloquent messages about the need to develop a positive habit of self-assertion, particularly when it's connected to a knowledge of one's own spiritual core.

A Modern Day Success with This Positive Habit

Jane and her husband had retired from corporate careers and hectic lives in Washington D.C. They wanted to find a mellower pace of life and a more beautiful setting for their retirement home, and they settled into a house on the Eastern Shore of Virginia, astride the Chesapeake Bay.

With this major life change, they suddenly found themselves with time to explore hobbies and interests. Jane's husband, Robert, spent many afternoons on the golf course adjacent to their neighborhood, perfecting his game with some of the other men in the community. Jane spent mornings on the beach with a huge straw hat and a good book.

The morning peace and quiet of the beach started her day on a positive note. She often noted how extraordinarily beautiful was the Chesapeake Bay, with its small islands just offshore and the glassy look of the water.

One day upon having just finished a novel and without another to read, she took a sketchpad down to the beach. At one time in her life, Jane had been a promising young artist, but that was during college. She had long ago left those talents behind when she started a family. Being an at-home mother had taken up quite a bit of time, and as soon as the youngest was in kindergarten, she had gone back to work full time. Her art was seemingly left in her past.

But that day at the beach, she decided to try to pick it up again. "I just started to draw one day. It had literally been decades since I had attempted to sketch anything worthwhile. But I was surprised how easily it came back, probably due to the fact that I had such a beautiful seascape to inspire me. It just flowed."

Sketching became Jane's favorite new pastime; she preferred it even to reading novels. She would walk up and down the shoreline of the Bay looking for different vistas or new wildlife. Sometimes she and her husband would take day trips, and he would fish while she would draw or paint.

"It felt so good to express myself creatively. It was like another side of myself that I was meeting for the first time in twenty years. I am at my most peaceful, most centered when I am on the beach with paints or charcoal."

One night in mid-September, while the weather was still warm, Jane and Robert had some new friends from the community over for dinner. Jane had been cooking all afternoon and forgot that she had left a painting on the back screen porch to dry. As the party finished dinner, they drifted outside to enjoy the bay views. Three of the women in attendance were local artists, and they gravitated toward the painting as soon as they walked out onto the porch. Jane, who enjoyed her work but did not have much confidence in her talents, was embarrassed and quickly took the painting inside. But the women followed her inside complimenting her work with enthusiasm beyond standard politeness.

They begged to see more. Reluctantly, Jane led them upstairs and into the study where she had about twenty paintings and charcoal sketches. The women were impressed. "Deborah and Suzanne were painters and Roxy was a basket-weaver. They were very excited about my work and wanted me to show it at an upcoming arts and crafts festival centering on the theme 'Marine Life.' I was flattered that they thought my work deserved to be shown to the public, but I had no idea how much my paintings were worth or how they would look hanging next to professional art work."

Jane accepted the invitation to show her work, but she was nervous. Her husband advised her to have a little faith in her abilities, but she knew this was easier said than done. She just didn't consider herself an artist. But with all the self-confidence she could muster and the show three weeks away, she began working tirelessly on her art.

The show was in Fairfax, Virginia, a suburb of Washington, D.C. Some of Jane's old friends from the city came to support her new endeavor, and she was pleased with their vote of confidence. Her artwork sold reasonably well—one piece on the first day, followed by three on the second day and two on the third.

Each day Jane's excitement increased and her confidence strengthened. Those positive feelings culminated when, on the afternoon of the last day, a photographer for a fishing magazine expressed interest in showcasing her work with other marine-inspired artists in a layout on the Chesapeake Bay. Now Jane really felt like an artist!

With this successful show behind her, Jane took the initiative to gather information about upcoming shows. She signed up along with Deborah for a show in Baltimore the next month. Jane poured all her time and energy into her artwork for the remainder of October. Her husband Robert was extremely supportive of his wife's new passion, even posing for a couple of the paintings.

At the same time that Jane was deeply entrenched in her preparation for the Baltimore show, her son, Alex, was planning marriage. Alex was her son from her first husband David; but the marriage had ended shortly after Alex was born, and the next year she had met Robert. Both her son and her first husband lived in Chapel Hill, North Carolina. Alex and Rachel, his wife-to-be, were planning an elaborate ceremony which would inevitably require extensive preparation. Naturally, Alex wanted the assistance and support of his parents in this hectic time. Jane contacted her ex-husband to discuss plans for the wedding, but their talk went rather badly.

David was still working as an insurance agent and was very busy that autumn as he had always been. He was, as any proud father would be, excited about the wedding; but he didn't have time to help with preparations. The way he saw it, Jane was retired, she had nothing to do, and she should come to North Carolina to provide assistance. Jane had never been particularly good at standing up to her ex-husband, not when they were married or now, thirty years later.

Jane listened on the phone to David; he did most of the talking. But when he made a statement that she had nothing to do with her time, she became angry. Jane had been working for hours every day, producing beautiful paintings that captured the true beauty of the Bay, and she deeply resented David's accusation that she was idle.

"I always have a hard time speaking my mind with my ex-husband. Perhaps because I was so young when we were married that I did not know myself well enough to have my own opinions. I'm not really sure why. I just kind of fell into that pattern with him. But that night on the phone, when we were speaking about Alex's wedding plans, I just had this spurt of assertiveness. Maybe it was because I was so proud of my shows and really feeling confident. I was direct with him, and that felt nice."

As David tried to free himself from responsibility to his son's plans, Jane stood up for herself in a way that she had never really done before. "I just told him, 'It makes me unhappy that you don't think my work is of any value. Just because I am retired from a corporate job does not mean I don't work. In fact, David, this art I'm doing is in many ways more demanding than any job I have ever held."

She paused, expecting a sarcastic comeback. But the phone was silent, so she continued because she did not know what else to do. "Alex just needs to feel that we are supportive of him. I speak with him on the phone almost every night, and he is excited about the artwork I am doing."

She stopped, but he was silent. Then he sighed and asked, "Where are you going with this, Jane?"

"You only live thirty minutes from Alex. I am headed for Baltimore tomorrow and when I am home, Chapel Hill is still half a day's drive away. I am not going to let you make me feel guilty for investing time in something that I love to do." David ended the conversation quickly. Jane realized later that he wasn't used to her being so direct about her emotions and priorities. He hadn't really known how to respond.

When Jane spoke with Alex the next week, she was surprised and happy to hear that David had gone to look at flatware with Alex and Rachel. What's more they had a lunch date planned to look at pictures of cakes from the baker. Both Alex and Rachel were pleased that David was taking such an interest in the wedding plans.

All of this was a new experience for Jane. She had not

only found confidence in her artistic abilities, she also had calmly and clearly expressed her feelings to her ex-husband with whom she rarely had positive conversations. She was quite proud of herself, and she was determined to better her life with this newfound confidence and ability to assert herself.

APPLYING THIS POSITIVE HABIT TO YOUR LIFE

Spend a week consciously practicing the healthy use of your will to be more self-assertive. Let it be loving, patient self-assertion. Stay focused on five ways in which this can happen for you: (1) sticking to decisions you've made (like the advice Cayce gave to the man who was so irresolute), (2) expressing positive feelings, (3) communicating negative feelings, (4) setting limits, and (5) taking initiatives.

You may feel more comfortable with some of these methods than with others. Or, you may find that the situations you encounter during the week clearly require some methods more than others. See what you learn about your best self—individuality—by this loving, firm, and creative approach to self-affirmation.

PICTURE YOURSELF

*Positive
Habit
#7*

Picture Yourself: Using Creative Visualization for Change

Advertising executives know about the power of visualization. They frequently encourage us to play with the mind and imagine a product or a place they'd like us to buy:

"Picture yourself in a brand new Mercedes . . . "

"Picture yourself as you look out from the balcony of your oceanfront Hawaiian condo . . . "

But how much impact can we really expect from imaginative creations of the mind? For example, does visualization merely program our own behavior, or does it also help to shape conditions beyond ourselves? This riddle is truly one of the "mysteries of the mind," as the Cayce readings on occasion referred to them.

A fundamental principle of life says, "Mind is the Builder." But what does that really mean? In order to explore that question in our own lives, we should first recognize that "mind" denotes more than merely logic and intellect. The creative part of us includes intuition, feeling, and imagination as well. In fact, a good way to test the principle "Mind is the Builder" is to explore visualization—a function of the mind that can make use of its many aspects.

Modern psychology knows something of the powers of

visualization. Introductory psychology courses often include illustrations of the mind's powers as documented in research with visualization and human performance. For example, in one study volunteers were pre-tested for their proficiency in making free throws on a basketball court. Half the group was then given the opportunity to practice on the court; the other half left the court and was guided through mental exercises in which they "practiced" by visualizing themselves successfully making shots. Then both groups were given a retest to see how well they could do with free throws. Remarkably, the group that had spent time off-court visualizing showed as much improvement as those that actually practiced with a basketball!

Of course, there is bound to be a point at which visualization can no longer substitute for physical behavior. No one is likely to become an instant professional basketball player by imagination alone. Nevertheless, psychological research like this suggests that we can do a lot to change ourselves for the better, simply by making use of this extraordinary talent called visualization. Many skilled athletes use it regularly to bring out their best—for example, a golfer who imagines the perfect swing and shot before picking up his club; or, a springboard diver who visualizes in advance the leap into the pool just the way she wants it to be. Even medical science—a field that has historically shied away from serious consideration of mind-body interaction—has become more and more open to the use of visualization in the treatment of illnesses such as cancer.

To better understand the life-affirming potentials of the technique called visualization, let's consider an even more fundamental topic: imagination. It's the actual capability of the human mind that's put to use when we practice visualization.

THE IMAGINATIVE FORCES

Use your imagination.

When are you likely to get that sort of advice? When you face a challenge in which the old ways don't seem to be working. When you're trying to do something creative. When you need to expand the boundaries of your thinking beyond the familiar.

What exactly is imagination or, as Cayce called it, "the imaginative forces"? It is probably one of the most celebrated human talents. A huge exhibit building at the Disney World's Epcot Center salutes the imagination, pointing out with dozens of examples how this faculty has played a significant role in our history.

Imagination is one of the mind's most significant capabilities, but there are many. As mentioned earlier, the mind has impressive versatility. It can process information in a linear, logical way. In fact, such rational analysis has been featured so strongly in modern society, that some people almost equate logical intellect with the mind itself. But there are other capabilities that are equally important. Memory is one. The human mind is an extraordinary storehouse in which is recorded every sensory impression, every thought, and every feeling of this lifetime.

Intuition is another capability of the mind. This includes psychic sensitivity, along with the ability to process subliminal perceptions and unconscious memories. It might be argued that intuition is a more mysterious process than rational analysis or memory. We can build computer mechanisms that do a good job replicating those other two mental faculties, but copying intuition is a far more difficult task.

Imagination is a close cousin of intuition. No doubt the mind makes use of its intuitive capabilities when it operates imaginatively. But what sets imagination apart from other mental powers is its creative function—its ability to fashion something new. When your imaginative forces are active, you get a taste of what might be called cocreativity. Not only is God the Creator, but we too are blessed with the ability to be creators, starting in the mental world. Sometimes that creativity means making something entirely new—for example, an original invention, a novel dessert recipe, or an unprecedented musical composition. On other occasions, the imaginative forces draw on memories and re-create vividly in the mental world.

Also closely related to imagination is yet another mental capacity: feeling. In this case the word refers not to the physical sense of touch but rather to our inner world of emotion. Imagination has a powerful influence on our feeling life. Imagining a trip to the dentist or a public speaking requirement can immediately stimulate feelings of fear in some people. Imagining a beach vacation can instantaneously awaken feelings of peace in other individuals. Feeling is a critical ingredient to effective meditation, and we might expect that purposeful, directed use of the imaginative forces would play a useful role in that spiritual discipline.

Ideals are another important topic when we try to understand imagination. Many passages in the Cayce material directly link ideals with the imaginative forces. For example, Cayce spoke about this to one thirty-six-year-old woman whose principal motive for getting a reading was concern about her future. His clairvoyant overview of her life began with a statement that she had not yet set a spiritual ideal. It went on to describe how "with an ideal, and not just an idea, there is the constant action from the mental, the imaginative, and the spiritual forces . . . " (5663-1)

In a similar way, Cayce advised a young woman who was contemplating marriage but didn't want to make a mistake. The reading (1243-1) instructed her to clarify her ideals and then take them into her prayer and meditation life, and into what was described as "daydreams." Here he seemed to be recommending a purposeful use of imagination and visualization—something that could be very constructive if used wisely. It can be an inner activity in which our ideals are allowed to express themselves imaginatively.

Perhaps the best illustration of this process is found in Cayce's suggestions to a nineteen-year-old man. He had received a physical reading four years earlier that had produced good results, and on this second occasion asked for vocational guidance. Cayce described an imaginative activity that the young man did occasionally: "At such periods the entity may lapse into what is sometimes called 'day dreaming.'" He was encouraged to continue this process but to make it somewhat more directed and purposeful, helping him to clarify his own ideals. Cayce continued, "It [the imaginative activity] is then given to formulate in the mind of self ideals, and even able to visualize or to word same somewhat in a poetic nature." (1664-2) Finally, the reading suggested that he add another element to this practice. Study the Bible and use these creative, imaginative forces meditatively to experience more deeply the meaning of these biblical messages. "And add to same much of that as may be gained, at such periods, from a study of the Word of Life, the Book, the Bible; meditating on those commands, those promises, those warnings."

THE KEYS TO VISUALIZATION

Some people have trouble getting excited about the possibilities of visualization because they don't think of themselves as very effective at "picture making." In other words, when they close their eyes they fail to see the vivid, three-dimensional movies which they erroneously assume almost everyone else sees. In fact, very few people are capable of getting visual images so clear and graphic. Most of us imagine in such a way that it has only vaguely a "visual" character. Perhaps more significant is the "feeling" engendered.

When you consciously try to imagine something—for example, if you attempt to visualize an excellent physical performance—you may get positive results, even if you aren't very skillful in conjuring up lifelike pictures. Most practitioners have found the success is more closely linked to the ability to feel the desired goal—in one's physical body *and* in what the Cayce readings called the mental body.

Another way in which feeling plays a role is motivation. The principle that "Mind is the Builder" means that a real thought-form is created each time we focus the mind. The vitality and strength of that thought-form is largely shaped by the intensity of feeling that goes into it. Sincerity and desire go a long way in allowing visualization to work effectively.

Of course, there is one catch when it comes to actually experiencing "Mind is the Builder." Although our physical experiences may be the result of what we've created with the mind, a time-lag exists between the mental creation and the physical manifestation. For example, if a man spends ten minutes each day visualizing success in his sales job, will it take a week, a year, or a lifetime before his boss will see measurable changes? Or, will the boss even know how to measure the kinds of changes that are taking place? These are elusive issues, and there's no simple rule that makes it easy to predict the timing.

In what way does the Cayce material actually *recommend* the use of visualization for creating a more centered physical, mental, and spiritual life? Clearly it describes the mechanics of how it works, but is there an endorsement to make such conscious efforts a positive habit? The answer is yes—but with some qualifications. One point of caution is to avoid the mistaken notion that visualization provides some sort of short cut. " . . . no short cuts in metaphysics, no matter what those say who would force by visualization . . . " is the way it was said to one man. (5392-1)

Another reservation is that visualization should not be used to manipulate the thoughts, feelings, or actions of someone else. It may well be *possible* to do so, but it's not in the best interest of that person or oneself. To do so would be to override the free will of that individual. And so, for example, we may be concerned that someone's behavior is self-destructive; but if that person hasn't asked us to do so, it would be inappropriate to visualize him changing his actions.

In spite of these qualifications, the Cayce material is generally encouraging about the positive potentials of visualization. It can bring benefits to ourselves. As he put it once, "Visualize, and you will make it and can use it to the advantage and the help of others." (5103-1) But the advantage it brings to others will come as we are more loving, creative, and spiritually centered ourselves.

Probably Cayce's most frequent reference to visualization concerns making it a positive habit in order to promote self-healing. One powerful approach to stimulate healing—a technique that can be used in conjunction with even mainstream medical advice—is a meditative exercise in which the individual imagines the desired changes happening in the body. One key to success with this exercise is sincerity. As Cayce once described the use of visualization for greater health: " . . . do these—not as of rote . . . " (4515-1) That is to say, have your heart in it. Another key that he emphasized was gaining conscious knowledge of how the body works in order to make visualization for healing more effective. In other words, studying a little anatomy might lead to better results with visualization for physical healing.

Another type of change can be a mental healing—the use of visualization to alter our attitudes, emotions, and behaviors. To experience how this can work, it's best to target a specific change that you want to make. Here are four possible changes that might lend themselves well to the influence of your imaginative forces.

1. Smiling more often in your interactions with people.

2. Listening more carefully to people as they speak to you.

3. Taking time everyday to exercise and enjoying it.

4. Immediately forgiving and not taking personally the words and/or deeds of others which might normally hurt or offend you.

As you try visualization to make a change like one of the examples above, keep in mind several important components to a good visualization session. Try to incorporate them every time you use the exercise:

1. Have a clear purpose and be sure it resonates to your highest spiritual values. As Cayce said to one woman about visualization, "Then, spiritualize and visualize purposes, in the manner in which the entity desires things to be done, and you'll have them done!" (3577-1) Each time you start to use the visualization method, ask yourself, "What's my purpose for wanting to create this specific change for my future?"

2. Close your eyes and create a clear mental image. Of course, "Mind is the Builder" works all the time, not just when you close your eyes. However, most people find that they can best focus attention for this inward, creative activity by momentary cutting off visual stimuli from the material world. Remember that some people are better than others at "seeing" pictures, but that the impact of visualization can work equally well for everyone.

How does one best go about creating a clear image? One way is simply to imagine success. Be specific. Visualize a specific situation in as much detail as you can. Exercise your free will, and with your imagination pick the attitude, emotion, and behavior that you desire.

Another method is to start with a memory. Recall a situation in which you *failed* to think, feel, or act according to your goal. Re-create the scene and events in your mind, but this time alter what you think, feel, or do.

3. Fill the image with feeling. It's one thing to halfheartedly visualize something, but quite another to sincerely *desire* what you imagine.

4. In the end, release the image—let go of expectations about when or how it will manifest. This is a tough one for many people. In fact, this fourth point creates one of those frustrating paradoxes of the spiritual path. On the one hand, it's important that you believe visualization works and sincerely desire the outcome; but, conversely, holding too rigid an expectation about the timing can block the process.

A good time to practice visualization might be at the end of your meditation periods, if you have them. However, you can practice your visualization exercise at *any* time during the day—whenever it's possible to get quiet and center for a few minutes.

Whenever you consciously try to activate this positive habit, watch for results but don't become preoccupied with them. Let go of attachments concerning *when* changes will come. Be patient with yourself and conditions. But also be willing to make some effort. Remember that visualization is not a short cut—it simply *assists* you in making the changes you desire and in reaching your goals. For example, suppose that you choose the third sample discipline given earlier—taking time everyday to exercise and enjoying it. Even with the visualization method applied daily, you're still going to need to make an effort to exercise. Visualization may make it easier, but it won't magically remove the need for you to use your free will. The same might be said of any part of your life in which you try to make positive use of visualization.

A Story from the Cayce Archives

Agnes was a medical secretary and worked in the office

of an osteopath. For several years she had been suffering from psoriasis, a skin condition about which doctors in the 1930s knew little. To complicate matters even more, Agnes was also bothered by anemia. She visited her doctors regularly, and even made a trip to be examined by a specialist at Johns Hopkins in Baltimore. But none of the doctors had an answer for her. "I was never able to get a straightforward analysis from my physician," she wrote in one letter.

In the fall of 1932, Agnes was troubled with a severe recurrence of psoriasis, and she went to Edgar Cayce for a health reading. She had a relationship with the Cayce family stemming from her friendship with Edgar and Gertrude Cayce's son Hugh Lynn. What's more she had received a life reading from Mr. Cayce a few years earlier and trusted his insights because of the wise spiritual advice she had gotten in that first reading. Now she took her daunting health problems to Cayce for help.

In the subsequent physical reading, Cayce's diagnosis was improper eliminations due to a disturbance in blood circulation. Because things were out of balance, her body was trying to get rid of toxins through the skin, resulting in the psoriasis. But a transformation of the condition was possible, he promised. Cayce described for Agnes a considerable list of health procedures and natural remedies to aid her healing process. But he added with emphasis that a *psychological approach* would also mean a lot to her health. The healing method involving the mind was creative visualization. As he put it:

> Keep that attunement in which the body-physical, imaginative, *and* spiritual, can visualize for each part of that that *develops* in the body *before* the mental, spiritual and imaginative forces of the body. Few people are able in the beginning to be as generally imaginative as the body! Hence the body should be

able, with a little visualization of that as is *desired* by the self, to create for itself that atmosphere, that environ, for *that* being acted upon! 1048-3

Cayce emphasized that for visualization to work optimally, Agnes needed some knowledge of her own anatomy—in other words, to know something about the organ systems she would be trying to influence with her visualizations. His advice went on:

> This requires the necessary knowledge of the body, of the mind, of that as is desired by the body. Then *with* that knowledge and the proper visualization, the *understanding* comes. Knowledge is not power unless it is that that may be applied by the body *having* the knowledge . . . Then, as for the body in visualizing itself in that that may bring about the proper coordination of eliminations in the system . . .

In graphic detail Cayce then described for her exactly how the visualization for healing might be experienced. The key principle here is the individual's capacity to "see it being accomplished."

> Then, see these functioning in such a manner as to bring about that desired, or see that taking place which is desired by the body. In circulation (This as a vision for the body, of that which is asked concerning) of the blood supply through [the] throat, head and neck, passes through those affected portions in the throat or tonsils. The *blood* is carried immediately from these to those portions of the system where eliminations must take place . . . see that being accomplished, as the heart pumps the blood *through* the throat, the lungs, the liver, the heart, to the extremities, to those parts affected, and you can feel the pul-

sation—see—as in this body through which the information comes . . .

After receiving the reading, Agnes set to work applying it as best she could. She studied some basic anatomy, just enough to understand the workings of her dysfunctional organs. She practiced the visualizations, just as Cayce had described. And in addition she found a doctor to administer the remedies that Cayce had prescribed. From the combined treatments, Agnes recovered from the severe outbreak of her psoriasis. Later she wrote, "Since that time, I have had no recurrences of the trouble worth recording, though it is not apparently entirely gone from my system." Although she knew that this condition was a point of vulnerability for her body—and probably always would be—she had experienced a holistic transformation of her ailment, with the mental discipline of visualization playing a central role.

A MODERN DAY SUCCESS WITH THIS POSITIVE HABIT

Matt's job often required business trips that would keep him on the road for a week or more. Although these journeys occurred only about every month or six weeks, they had become huge distractions—even disruptions—in his life. Just when it seemed that he had settled into smooth routines at home and the office, it was time for another one of these trips.

It wasn't so much that he disliked the travel itself or the people that he would meet in distant places. All that was fine. But there were so many details to attend to, so many little things that had to be arranged. Something always seemed to go wrong somewhere long the line. Unless he put large amounts of time and thought into his preparations, the trip was likely to go awry, and the purposes of the travel could be thwarted.

Three weeks before he was scheduled for yet another of these business journeys, he was reading an article in a magazine of a doctor's waiting room. It described the power of mind that could be experienced via visualization and imagination. It occurred to him that trip-planning was the perfect place to test the idea in his own life. "Why not visualize all the details going just right? It seemed like a sure-fire way for me to experiment with what the article was promising. I just decided that for each upcoming day before the next trip—for only about five minutes—I would go over in my mind all the little steps involved in making the next trip go perfect—airline connections, rental car pick-ups, the weather, the quality of my meetings."

Matt was diligent in keeping the visualization exercise each morning. And as the departure day approached, he was actually looking forward to leaving, fairly confident that the trip was going to turn out to be a breeze. But, in fact, things didn't quite turn out that way. At the end of the six-day excursion, he wrote, "I can see now that the visualizations in advance did make some important differences. Simply having gone through all the details of the trip in my imagination had helped me prepare myself, and my meetings in particular seemed to go better than anyone would have anticipated. But other parts of the trip weren't so hot. There was a missed flight connection and one car rental company kept trying to force me into a different rate plan than I knew I had reserved."

The whole thing made Matt doubt just how malleable the future is to visualization. He talked the experience over with a friend the next week. It was someone who had a long history of working with intuition and deeper levels of the mind, and Matt wanted to know if this friend could enlighten him on the apparent failure. It was from this friend that Matt learned a little bit different approach to using visualization to optimize his travel. The change was to give higher priority to imagining things about his inner life. He needed to visualize the best inner reactions and responses to the kinds of challenges that might come up during a long trip.

With another business journey scheduled for the coming month, Matt decided to give it another try. As before, he practiced visualizing each morning the various logistics of his itinerary. Although he tried to imagine them going smoothly, he paid special attention to seeing himself as patient and tolerant with whatever might arise and good humored about the various adventures that might face him on the road. This new set of visualizations, in other words, became more about Matt's inner life and less about outer events. The results were striking the following month as the trip unfolded. He wrote afterwards, "Just like the previous trip there were some things that went wrong. This time it wasn't a missed connection, but I had a less-than-desirable seat on one long flight and my room wasn't ready for me at one hotel when I tried to check in at 4:00 p.m. But I was able to stay pretty loose about the whole thing and just take everything in stride. It was as if my visualizations and imaginations had made it easier for me to be mellow and simply go with the flow." Needless to say, from the lessons of this second effort Matt had discovered a powerful, positive habit to apply to many aspects of his life, not just business trips.

Applying This Positive Habit to Your Life

Experiment with the principle "Mind is the Builder" in your own life. For a week, try to be especially conscious of the power of creative visualization and imagination. But always remember that the "fruits" of our efforts sometimes don't manifest in only seven days. Nevertheless, you can still watch for some evidence of the positive impact of purposeful visualization, even during a personal project as short as this one.

You will use the visualization exercise to target a specific change that you want to make. First, identify something in yourself that you want to alter—perhaps an attitude or emotion you want to express more frequently or less frequently. Or maybe it will be a behavior you want to emphasize, such as "smiling more often," an example given earlier.

The method itself takes only two or three minutes each time you use it. Set aside a few minutes daily to get relaxed, close your eyes, and purposefully direct your imaginative forces. Remind yourself of your purpose for wanting to make this change. Experience a connection with that motivation.

Then, move into the actual visualization, in whatever form that seems to work best for you. "See" yourself being successful with your intention. Infuse that set of images with feeling, both the sincerity of your desire *and* how you feel when you are successful with your intention.

In those two or three minutes, you may want to practice several scenes or imaginary situations of success. And then, finally, let it all go. Release any expectations or any sense of compulsion about the intended changes and just trust that something purposeful has been set in motion.

Throughout the week, during all the times you are not engaged in the visualization exercise, be ready and willing to do your part to make the desired intentions come true. Apply a little effort with your will. See if the changes start coming a little more easily because of the creative visualization discipline that you have been keeping.

Positive
Habit
#8

Tolerance: The Magic
Ingredient in Human Relationships

Human relations. They probably cause the most pleasure and the most difficulty of any part of living. It's no wonder that problems with relationships were one of the most frequent issues brought to Edgar Cayce—second only to health concerns. Almost every imaginable kind of dilemma between people was submitted to Cayce for his intuitive advice. Marriage, divorce, parenting, work relations, friendships, rivalries. It's all there. And if there's any one secret in what he had to say, it's this: Getting along with people requires tolerance.

Tolerance is an elusive quality, and it isn't easy to find in today's world. Nor was it in Cayce's time. As he said in one woman's reading: "So few souls or entities have combined love in the material plane with tolerance! For, love in the material becomes egotistical, and this is opposite from tolerance." (2629-1)

Tolerance requires a forgiving spirit. It means a willingness to dismiss something that seems wrong or unfair. When we're tolerant, we give other people the benefit of the doubt—or, as the popular saying goes, we "cut them a little slack."

Tolerance requires a certain "flexibility of spirit." It allows things to keep going, even when someone hasn't exactly measured up to what they ought to be, or even could be with a little more effort. Think about tolerance in terms of how the word is used in mechanical engineering. It is the measure of how much deviation is acceptable. For example, in the manufacturing of a door and its frame, the cuts might have a tolerance of one-eighth inch. As long as the production errors are no larger, the door will operate smoothly. But to exceed that tolerance level means problems.

Our lives, just like the door, need balanced, healthy tolerance. How much flexibility have you built into your way of meeting the world? Are you so inflexible that you get "jammed," or do you have enough "give" to continue functioning in spite of imperfections?

Unfortunately we often fall short and don't exhibit much of this positive habit. For example, just because we care about someone doesn't necessarily mean that we've learned how to be tolerant. If Cayce is correct about material world experience, our loving concern easily becomes "egotistical." In other words, we tend to let biases, personal expectations, and rigidity make us intolerant; and this intolerance can strain our most important relationships or prevent us from forming new ones.

Consider for the moment the psychology of "intolerance." What goes on inside of us when we're not getting along with others and we're highly critical? Our judgmental, impatient feelings usually make a lot of sense, given the circumstances. In fact, what makes tolerance so rare is the illogic of it. With minds that are usually alert for faults and inconsistencies, we're inclined to pounce on the shortcomings of competitors and strangers, not to mention family, friends, and colleagues. We hold those individuals strictly accountable. We're quick to react—inwardly or outwardly—to their slip-ups and errors. Maybe we become intolerant because we feel as if other people are always looking over our shoulders, watching for our own mistakes. It may be a hard-nosed boss, a demanding spouse, or a faultfinding parent. And so we recycle the intolerance.

But to have satisfying and healthy relationships, we've got to find a way to break that cycle. To survive in a world of strong opinions and fierce competition, we must learn and practice the positive habit of tolerance. Those who master the skill will find it much easier to stay spiritually centered, *and* they will benefit greatly our global society that so desperately needs more tolerance.

DEALING WITH HUMAN DIFFERENCE AND INDIVIDUALITY ON THE GLOBAL SCENE

For the twenty-first century, tolerance will be a key issue for the human family. No opportunity is likely to be more important than the one that humanity faces to find new ways of getting along with each other. Surely this is the century of human relations on an international scale. Every place on the national and international scene would benefit remarkably by greater human tolerance.

Overpopulation forces this need to center stage. Already the numbers are reaching explosive proportions, and the countries of the world are straining their resources. By all accounts, we are headed toward doubling the number of people on the planet by 2050! Increasing numbers of people bring challenges not only about food, housing, and public health. There is also the fundamental issue of how people interact with each other. And these *social* opportunities may be the most difficult ones.

Probably only tolerance can keep this fast-changing world from coming apart at the seams. Hope for a healthy global society depends on people learning to be respectful and tolerant of each other. We must find ways to deal with differences and conflict in a constructive way. It's increasingly inevitable that each of us—on a nearly daily basis—will have to deal with people we find offensive or misguided. The question becomes, "Can we be tolerant and still live what we know to be doing ourselves?"

More people means more ideas, points of view, and beliefs. We are going to be rubbing shoulders with a more diverse group of people in our lifetime than past generations did. And how will we deal with all these people? Will we be able to live harmoniously when opinions differ so greatly?

In many ways the technological revolution is making the tensions within these differences even more volatile. The media make people's ideas vastly more accessible than ever before. Especially with the Internet, we are moving toward a situation of almost universal accessibility to largely unregulated (and unverified) information about people and their interests.

Consider what can happen even today with just a few minutes spent online with the worldwide web. Your computer screen is likely bombarded by promotions and advertisements for diverse sites, many of them not very closely in line with your own ideas and ideals. And while the Internet offers the newest and largest collection of information, increased availability of information about diverse opinions comes through other media, like books and brochures. Desktop publishing allows anyone with a computer to create publications that not so long ago could be done only by professionals and at great expense. Digital television with hundreds of channels will be creating an around-the-clock medium through which opinions are expressed and products are sold.

None of this is all bad or all good. There are obvious benefits to having information at our fingertips. There are great benefits to being able to log onto the Internet and find the most obscure facts without even leaving the living room. Electronic connectivity is changing the way we communicate with one another—for example, allowing us inexpensively to keep in touch with long distance friends and relatives through e-mail. Computers allow students newer and faster means of research and publication. Technology is making society more informed and universal. The same products are being marketed in Tokyo and Iowa, in Brazil and Iceland; and business is done between them in the blink of an eye, breaking down barriers of language and culture.

But as we get used to a faced-paced, globalized society, we must be careful to retain our individuality and remember to honor the same in others. And to make matters even more tricky, learning how to live with spiritual centeredness in the twenty-first century requires dealing with a strange paradox. On the one hand, society is becoming more homogenous; but at the same time, individuals are demanding their right to autonomy and the freedom of expression.

As people become more adamant about expressing themselves as individuals, how do we deal with the differences of opinion in the world? Do we have a right to express beliefs that we know will offend others? With an expanding population, the ability to deal in a healthy manner with difference of opinion will become even more necessary. And one way to do this is to make respectful tolerance a positive habit in our daily lives.

THE ASPECTS OF TOLERANCE

As a positive habit that can be learned and mastered, we can enhance tolerance by looking carefully at some of its features. Cayce highlighted several specific aspects of tolerance:

Forgiveness. The very essence of tolerance is a forgiving spirit, a willingness to put offenses and hurts aside. This doesn't mean excusing or accepting harmful behavior. Instead, it's a matter of disapproving of bad behavior without disapproving of the person. Forgiveness starts with the ability to recognize people's shortcomings, but at the same time to see their positive sides, as well.

Forgiveness can be as simple as putting aside differences with a friend or co-worker. But sometimes the challenge is far more difficult because the issue is much more deep-rooted. In the case of an extremely hurtful situation, forgiveness can end up taking months, years, and even lifetimes, unless a conscious, focused effort is made.

No matter what the scale of the injury, offense, or wound, forgiveness can be practiced on a small level each day. Work your way up to the more difficult issues. Start using forgiveness in your daily life with strangers as well as loved ones.

Often when Cayce counseled people to nurture the positive habit of tolerance, forgiveness was the feature he called to mind. For example, one woman was told that she had a special ability for tolerance, and it equipped her to be an especially forgiving individual. Whether or not you consider yourself to be innately tolerant, the second half of Cayce's message to her had universal significance. "For, as indicated, the ability for the application of love as related to tolerance is the greater virtue in the entity's present experiences. Thus in thy dealings with others, magnify their virtues, minimize their faults. For, even as thy Lord condemned no one, even as He forgave, so would you forgive." (2629-1)

Nonjudgment. Refraining from judgment is closely related to forgiveness. Both involve avoiding condemnation. But whereas forgiveness is usually linked to personal affronts, nonjudgment is more far-reaching. Forgiveness is what we strive for when we have been individually hurt, but nonjudgment is needed in many cases when there has not even been a personal offense. For example, we may find ourselves being judgmental and intolerant of people based solely upon their lifestyle, values, and beliefs.

Any kind of condemnation rarely if ever serves our own best interests or those of the other person. A judgmental attitude will only make our lives harder now and in the future. We cannot control the lifestyles of others, nor often can we do much to eliminate having to deal directly or indirectly with such people. Whether we like it or not, the choice often boils down to spending our energy disapproving of what we do not agree with *or* being nonjudgmental and tolerant.

Cayce had a distinct point of view about judgmental intolerance: It is not only detrimental to the target of our censure but to ourselves as well. It tends to undermine our own spiritual and physical health. In a reading given to the original Search for God Study Group, the following principle was proposed: " . . . judge not others, condemn not others. This is not love divine, neither is it wisdom. For it builds barriers, it destroys, it undermines the life of self first . . . " (262-104)

Broad-mindedness. Tolerance sees a place for everyone's point of view; and it has a breadth of vision that leaves room for many perspectives. But this sort of broad-minded tolerance is frequently difficult to pull off. We live in a confrontive, contentious society. And because of this combative climate, we can erroneously slip into believing that it's a weakness to appreciate someone else's line of reasoning. However, in order to live the positive habit of tolerance, we must escape from the power of those misconceptions. It's possible to hold onto one's own beliefs while at the same time having sympathetic appreciation for those of someone else.

Here's a way to experiment with this sort of broad-minded tolerance. Try to imagine what is going on in someone else's mind—that person's ideas and thought patterns. To do this, you must momentarily suspend your own reasoning and put yourself in that other person's shoes.

Of course, a desire to understand the thinking of someone else doesn't require that you permanently surrender your own point of view. This exercise in appreciation may occasionally end up making you want to amend your own thinking, in which case you will have benefited from your broad-mindedness. But perhaps even more often, you won't change your stance after considering the position of another person. Either way, the exercise will help you get along better with that person. Broad-mindedness is not only a means by which to tolerate others, it is also a chance for you to learn and test your opinions.

Cayce spoke directly about broad-mindedness as a universally desirable quality. He described one man with, " . . . broadness of the vision; the ability to meet conditions in the material plane in a manner that *all* are given their due consideration . . . and a lesson that has been gained by the soul of this entity of tolerance may be one that may be desired by all." (555-1) It's a positive habit worth any of us striving for!

Refraining from Arguments. Whereas the first three features of tolerance—forgiveness, nonjudgment, and broad-mindedness—are more inward experiences, the fourth feature is reflected most directly in our outer behaviors. Intolerance easily leads to disputes. Almost automatically we fall into arguments, big and small.

We may well find that with self-control we can overcome the compulsion to argue and enter into verbal sparring matches. Think about the pivotal moment that seems to come inwardly whenever we are on the verge of a disagreement. There is usually a point at which we feel we are being pushed beyond our breaking point. In that instant, we either fall into an argument or we heed the little voice in us that says "Stay calm." That voice, that small impulse, is the essence of tolerance. If tolerance is given the opportunity to grow, it can turn into forgiveness, nonjudgment, and broad-mindedness. But first that seed has to be given an opportunity, and succumbing to the compulsion to argue is the surest way to cut it off.

In this sense, we can say that restraining ourselves from

needless argument is a good starting point for developing tolerance, especially for any of us who have strong inclinations for intolerance. Particularly this may be the case for people who often feel very sure of themselves. Cayce pointed this out to one woman, saying that she "oft tends to become argumentative with those who disagree. Hence the lesson to be learned in this experience is more that of tolerance. Arguments will seldom change the aspects or the views of any." (1669-1)

POTENTIAL DISTORTIONS OF TOLERANCE

As strongly as tolerance is recommended, it is not a perfect virtue. Tolerance can go wrong or be used out of balance. For example, there are times when we need to speak up or challenge someone. If we are using tolerance as a way of avoiding conformation, we may be creating even bigger problems for ourselves. When those occasions arise, we can use confrontation in a constructive manner, and maintain our respect for the other person. In other words, we can practice tolerance without being a "pushover."

Another potential misuse of tolerance is more subtle. What could Cayce have meant when he said to one woman, "One may be tolerant and yet self-indulgent . . . "? (1298-1) Could it be that sometimes we are tempted to pat our selves on the back for how forgiving, broad-minded, and tolerant we are? Could this be the sort of inappropriate self-indulgence against which Cayce warns?

Or maybe it is something even more difficult to detect. Sometimes, if we aren't careful, we may *seem* to be tolerant of someone, but our apparent patience or restraint is actually self-serving. The classic illustration of this misuse is the codependent relationship. Suppose the wife is the main breadwinner in the marriage. The husband has shop-o-holic tendencies; and, since he doesn't work outside of the home, he relies on his wife to provide the money for his sports equipment addiction. The wife is "tolerant" of her husband's sometimes outrageous spending. What appears to be a virtue on her part, may be a self-serving form of tolerance. Perhaps, either unconsciously or consciously, the wife tolerates the overspending because it keeps her in control of the marriage or simply makes her feel needed.

The potential misuses of tolerance shouldn't keep us from seeing just how critical an ingredient it is in relationships and just how crucial it is in our dealing with strangers. Tolerance is a powerful tool in getting along with others, and in this new century, we will be spiritually lost without it.

A Story from the Cayce Archives

Michelle was a fifty-year-old woman from Belgium who had worked as a teacher for most of her adult life. In 1941 when she contacted Edgar Cayce for some life guidance, she was working in a small private school as a teacher and counselor. Mademoiselle Michelle—as she was called by her students because of her French-speaking ancestry and accent—loved her work and formed close friendships with the children she taught.

Years earlier she had become so trusted by the children that the school principal had asked her to serve as the school's first guidance counselor, in addition to her duties as the French teacher. Though the new position required quite a bit of extra work, Michelle had been eager to provide assistance to the children she loved. Students would make appointments with her for the hour after school, and she would advise them to the best of her ability on academic and personal matters.

Michelle contacted Cayce for advice because she felt perplexed about whether or not she was doing the right thing with her life. She had never married or had her own family, and she wasn't sure she had followed the right life path. Also, she was worried about her own personality characteristics, especially her tendencies to see the best in other people. Was it really a serious weakness, masked as an apparent virtue?

There was one school family in particular with which Mademoiselle Michelle felt a special closeness, and she wanted Cayce's opinion on the reasons for this affinity. The family had two girls and two boys, all four of whom attended the school. The youngest girl had an amazing grasp on the French language and Michelle had struck up a friendship with the mother discussing her daughter's talents. Anytime Michelle thought about leaving her teaching post, she was overcome by the sad prospects of leaving this family.

But Michelle's own childhood family was not satisfied with her choices in life. Her mother still wanted to see Michelle marry. Her brothers did not understand why Michelle cared to stay at this teaching job when she could find work with a higher salary. Though Michelle was happy with her life, her family's persistence made her doubt herself. And so, she contacted Cayce for advice, hoping to gain some clearer sense of direction.

In November 1941 Cayce gave a reading for Michelle that answered her questions and eased some of her doubts. He addressed her skills with people, especially children. " . . . God so loved the world as to give His only begotten Son. So has this entity so loved its fellow man as to give itself, its life, its abilities, its virtues, that others might know—too—that God is mindful of them." (2629-1)

Cayce thought that Michelle's dedication to the education of children was a very noble way to spend her life. He saw no reason for her to quit because teaching was a valuable way for Michelle to make use of her talents. What's more, she possessed a rare ability for tolerance—one that was both loving *and* able to give people the space and understanding that they need. "In Jupiter we find the universality, the ability for being tolerant. So few souls or entities have combined love in the material plane with tolerance! For, love in the material becomes egotistical, and this is the opposite from tolerance."

It was her ability to be tolerant of others that allowed her to see the good in people rather than the negative. In working with children it was important to keep in mind the positive so as to help them excel. Cayce thought Michelle's tendency to see only the good in people was a virtue and not something that made her weak, as she had feared.

"Thus in thy dealings with others, magnify their virtues, minimize their faults. For, even as thy Lord condemned no one, even as He forgave, so would you forgive. Even as thou counseled with those in that period, acting as the teacher, the instructor, in the abilities for practical application of life and to meet same in others."

Michelle asked Cayce about her friendships with the students. How greatly should she value them? He answered, "Here we find a wonderful contribution has been, the purposes never questioned, and the relationships should not be altered until there appears other activities for the entity. For, seemingly from nowhere, there will come material things to be used by the entity in this experience. These may alter the relationships in this school. In the present, be not afraid. Be mindful of those purposes, laying the stress in its proper sphere—as has been indicated—for the individual instruction, individual counsel, that has been and will be yet for a period."

Cayce did not rule out the possibility of Michelle having other means of expressing her talents other than as a teacher. But her ability to be tolerant made her a positive influence in the lives of many children, and she should not forget the importance of this work. Cayce added to the reading, "Ye have loved, ye do so love thy fellow man as to give thy mind, thy body, in counsel, in instruction, in those activities that enable the individual souls to think better of themselves and the reason thereof." (2629-1)

A Modern Day Success with This Positive Habit

Daniel was sixty-one-years old and looking forward to retirement in a few years so that he and his wife could travel. At his age he had decided just to try to be content with his line of work, even though changes were swirling around him. "I had been at my current job for seventeen years when my company decided to overhaul its computer operating systems. It meant lots of unexpected work and adaptation for the staff, but in the end it allowed me to have a real breakthrough. Thinking back about it now, five years later, its funny how one situation can change a person's view of a whole group of people."

The new computers were brought into their offices, and almost none of the staff knew how to use their more sophisticated software efficiently. At first it all seemed like a waste of money to buy equipment that no one knew how to use. The staff had been rather old-fashioned in relying principally on handwritten documentation and only occasional computer records, and now management wanted everyone to move up to the state-of-the-art. Each staff member got a couple of hours of training, but it was just enough to cover the basics.

That first week everyone in Daniel's department was highly stressed. It was a particularly busy time of year, and on top of performing their regular work, they had to fend for themselves with the new software. The general attitude at the office was one of frustration and annoyance. Before long management saw that the staff was unable to function effectively, and the following Monday, management responded with outside help. But it came in an unusual and unexpected package.

Three kids who didn't look to be older than eighteen were seen wandering around the halls. In what was normally a formal business setting, two were wearing khakis and one was wearing jeans. None of them wore ties. Daniel thought that maybe they were interns from the local community college, or perhaps one was a co-worker's son and his friends. Either way, Daniel didn't like how they waltzed around from office to office as if they belonged there. By the afternoon of their first day, it was common knowledge that these "kids" were only high school graduates who were not in the office to learn from experienced workers. They were the ones who had been hired to straighten out the computer problems! In spite of the nearly universal skepticism, they quickly began to show their worth.

"In the afternoon of the first day that these kids were hanging out at the office, my computer screen froze. When I had left for lunch, I had kept on-screen the master spreadsheet for the new departmental budget. It had taken me the better part of the morning to complete. Coming back from lunch, I sat down at my desk and the little arrow wouldn't budge when I moved the mouse. Sadly, I hadn't saved my work just before leaving for lunch. I figured these new machines were sure to be reliable, even if I was still just getting used to their new software. It was a big mistake on my part."

But the kids fixed his problem in a matter of minutes, even managing to retrieve his morning's work. As the teenagers left his office, one named Mike made a comment, "If you wanted to hang onto your work, you needed to have made sure you saved it." Of course Daniel wanted to have saved his work! Did they think he was doing all this tedious budget work just for fun? A part of him realized that Mike was just trying to be helpful and that he probably didn't know how to speak to adults in a business setting with respect. But overall, the encounter made Daniel feel even more annoyed and impatient with the boys.

In the next few days Daniel had several more negative encounters with the young computer consultants. He thought they were out of place in their confidence and didn't really understand what important work was going on there at the company. Daniel found their tactics of diagnosing and fixing problems to be careless and rather cavalier. What if they were wrong? This wasn't a high school geometry class. If they erased the wrong file, it would have big implications for Daniel's work. "Discretion is not one of my virtues. After having the kids around for a week, everyone in the office knew what I thought about them. Except for that one episode with my computer screen freezing, I never asked them for help. As far as I was concerned, they were unqualified and rude." All three teenagers knew that Daniel did not like them, and out of his earshot they had even referred to him as the "grumpy old man by the mailboxes."

After the teenage consultant had been part of the office scene for about a week, Daniel was sick on a Monday, and so that Tuesday he was very busy catching up. He had decided to work through lunch and had packed himself a sandwich as he left home that morning. It was twelve-thirty and he hadn't gone to the employee refrigerator to get his food yet, when Brett, one of the teenagers, walked past Daniel's open door. Brett backed up and came into the office, inquiring if Daniel was going to take a lunch break.

"I told Brett that I had a lot of work to do because I had been out of the office the day before. I turned back to my work, thinking he would leave, but he sat down on the other side of my desk. He asked me if I would like him to pick me up something at the Italian sandwich place down the street. I said, 'No thanks,' and he left."

The computer whiz Brett came back ten minutes later carrying two huge sandwiches, chips, and two soft drinks. He came into Daniel's office, telling Daniel that when you are getting over having been sick you need to eat to get your strength back.

Daniel asked Brett why he wasn't eating with his two

friends. Brett said that the other two had been working on the main server, and they had gone off to lunch without him. Daniel ate the sandwich, chips, and drink that Brett had unexpectedly brought back, even though he secretly would have preferred to be eating the sandwich he had packed for himself that morning.

Daniel thought about Brett's generous gesture the whole afternoon. Daniel acted like it was no big deal, but in actuality he was touched by it. Near the end of that work day, he made up some trivial computer difficulty and went looking for Brett. The two other boys were surprised to see Daniel's head peek through their makeshift cubicle. Brett followed Daniel back to his office to look at the problem. They had a nice chat about the computers and the speed with which the whole staff was picking up on the new computer usage. Daniel was pleased to learn that all three boys thought the computer programs were very complicated to learn; it eased Daniel's feelings of incompetence.

Three days later Daniel and Brett went down to the Italian sandwich shop for lunch together. Daniel received a few "I-thought-you-hated-these-kids" looks from coworkers, but he just smiled at them. Over lunch the two of them talked, and Daniel began to be open to a new perspective about Brett, one that allowed him to start feeling much more tolerant and accepting. In fact, Brett was quite at bit like Daniel had been when he was eighteen. Brett had done excellent work in high school, but when it came time for college, the money wasn't there. Daniel knew that story firsthand. Just like Daniel had done nearly forty years earlier, Brett was taking a year or two off in order to work and save money before beginning his undergraduate studies. Brett knew a lot about computers, and this kind of informal consultant work sure beat working at a fast food restaurant.

With this extra and more personal knowledge about Brett, Daniel found it easy to forgive behaviors from the last week that had initially annoyed or offended him. Even more amazing was the feeling and attitude that this lunchtime discussion stimulated in Daniel toward the other two boys—and even teenagers in general. The whole episode had put him back in touch with some of his own struggles and accomplishments when he was that age. It gave him a much more nonjudgmental frame of reference in which tolerance replaced annoyance and frustration.

The young computer consultants left the following week for another company in need of their services, and Daniel never saw Brett again. But he did see teenagers; they were everywhere. On the road, they drove like maniacs, blasting their music. In the neighborhood they had parties and were generally boisterous. But Daniel, instead of silently cursing them, thought of all of them as if they were Brett— nice kids underneath. He might not understand them, and he often didn't like their behavior. But that was okay. He could tolerate them, just like he and Brett had developed a tolerant respect for each other.

APPLYING THIS POSITIVE HABIT TO YOUR LIFE

As an experiment in tolerance at a personal level, look for ways that you can start living this important trait more consciously for the twenty-first century. Look for places close to home. Maybe it means respecting a difference of opinion between you and another family member. Maybe it means "cutting a little slack" for the neighbor who has a noisy cookout.

Look for ways in which tolerance allows you to be more respectful of the individuality of another person, and find ways that you can exhibit the positive habit of greater flexibility of spirit. (You may even be pleasantly surprised at the responses you get!)

THE 6TH SENSE IN SLEEP

Positive
Habit
#9

Sixth Sense in Sleep

Sleep is the mysterious period each night that refreshes the body while the mind stays active. Where does your mind go while your physical self is asleep?

Some mornings when you awake there may be no clues. The past seven or eight hours may be a complete blank. But on other mornings, you may have the feeling that you have been out and about during the night. Perhaps you awake with a better attitude about a problem that you were pondering the night before. Or, perhaps a certain emotion is strongly on your mind.

Often, you probably wake up with the strongest clue of all that your inner self has been active during the night—the remembrance of a dream. Even if the events seem bizarre or indecipherable, a dream is the most obvious evidence pointing to the fact that you have had experiences while your physical body rested.

It is a different world into which the mind travels each night. Our dream life is not governed by the same part of us that shapes our familiar, waking life. Rather, it is a period of experience in which our unconscious mind is able to completely run the show while our conscious mind is immobilized.

The conscious mind's daily awareness is made up

largely of the input we receive from our five senses—seeing, hearing, tasting, smelling, and touching. But as we drift off to sleep at night, the physical senses no longer play such an influential role in creating our reality. It is when the five senses are minimized, as in sleep, that the *sixth sense*—our intuition—is able to be the guide.

There are two primary periods when the sixth sense in sleep offers guidance. First is during the course of the night as our dreams are filled with insights unimaginable to the waking senses. But sometimes this avenue is stymied or partially blocked. We may awaken with only fragments of dreams hovering in our memory or nothing at all.

These are the days when we especially want to pay attention to a second fruitful period for catching the workings of our sleeping intuition. In those few moments *between* full sleep and full wakefulness, we can have insights that are equally valuable and often easier to remember than dreams. Great rewards can come from listening to what is presented to us in this "hypnagogic" state. To make full use of our sixth sense in sleep we must be able to understand its guidance in either of the two forms.

THE SIXTH SENSE IN DREAMS

In Cayce's recommendation of positive habits for staying connected to our spiritual center, few subjects carry as much emphasis as dreams. In fact, he believed that dreams are real experiences with the potential to change us in the same ways that events do in our waking lives. Our dreaming mind is a vast storehouse of information accessible only when we are free of the confinements of our five wakeful senses. It is a habit of spiritually centered people to make use of that wealth of information to enhance their waking lives.

In order to make use of our dreams, we must be able to decipher the sixth sense wisdom that is coming through.

Ask yourself the following three questions to discover how your dreams can give you insights into your life. Each question is an interpretation method.

Method #1: How am I different from having this dream? The change is most likely to come in the form of a new attitude or different perspective. For example, a man brought a dream to Cayce for interpretation. It was a disturbing dream in which he was beating his wife and eventually killed her. The dream ended with him begging her to come back to life, promising he would be more sympathetic and understanding. Cayce's interpretation did not require analysis by symbols. Instead, he encouraged the man to look at the dream as a real experience within his soul—one that had changed his feelings and attitudes toward his wife.

In waking life he had not been violent, and he had no inclination of being so in the future. But he *had* been neglectful. And the morning he had awakened from that dream, he was a different man than the night before. The dream experience *itself* had stimulated an inner resolve to be more attentive and sympathetic. That in itself was the meaning; there was no need to decode any symbols. The meaning was in the change of feelings.

Such "feelings transformative dreams" can be some of the best examples of the sixth sense presenting its wisdom while we sleep. They are especially effective in helping us maintain a centered and healthy posture toward life, particularly in our relationships. Cayce certainly knew the value of gaining a new perspective through dreams. As he told another dreamer, "In dreams . . . each individual soul . . . reviews or sees as from a different attitude those experiences of its own activities." (257-136) In the midst of daily life, we can often get stuck in destructive routines that are difficult to break. Often dreams can give us a much-needed "fresh outlook," and we can emerge from sleep with more positive responses to unhealthy habits.

Method #2: How might this dream balance some extreme? In order for dreams to help us with waking life, we must understand them by learning to "speak their language." And sometimes that language is a kind of exaggeration or overstatement in order to make a point.

Because balance is so vital to a healthy, centered life, dreams can push us toward greater equilibrium in their effort to help us toward the needed balance. For example, in response to some extremely strong feeling or behavior in waking life, dreams can evoke the *opposite* response. To see and understand the dream's wisdom, ask yourself this simple question, "How might this dream balance some extreme?"

The extreme you discover in the dream can be an attitude, emotion, or action. It can be on the part of yourself (the dreamer) or another character in the dream (who probably represents you anyway). Then ask yourself if this extreme condition in the dream is actually the mirror opposite of an attitude, feeling, or way of acting in your daily life. If so, then this is probably your sixth sense and its intuitive wisdom trying to coax you back toward a greater balance in that part of your life. It is not, however, an invitation to go off to the opposite extreme from your daily life tendency. It is just a reminder (sometimes not too gentle) to find that balance point. As one Cayce reading put it, "Oft [dreams] may be as opposite that which is presented to the body . . . " (1968-10)

One classic example of this type is one that may come to a shy, withdrawn person who dreams that he or she is naked in a public place. The total exposure of this rather extreme behavior (extreme, at least for our culture) is *not* direct guidance to disrobe in public. Instead, the dream is a call to equilibrium and balance in regard to being more disclosing and demonstrative with one's thoughts and feelings. It points to the person's need to take more risks or find a way of interacting with others more openly.

Sometimes this so called "compensatory approach" to dream interpretation helps us understand those dreams that contain powerful emotions. A dream in which there is a display of explosive anger might reflect a person's tendency for repression. Some frightful dreams can indicate that one has been too complacent about a genuine threat, and that a more healthy respect for danger is needed. When you have a dream in which there is an extreme, think about how it relates to your wakeful life in terms of a call to be more balanced.

Method #3: What might this dream be telling me about my body? Our dreams are products of an intuitive mind that is always alert for what could lead to greater physical health. Spiritually centered people know how important it is to have the physical body as vital as possible, and they use their dreams to gain insight into the workings of the body. One of the most important contributions to the Cayce dream interpretation readings is an appreciation for "somatic dreams"—nocturnal experiences which symbolically describe or diagnose physical conditions in the dreamer's body.

There is no foolproof method of recognizing somatic dreams. However, certain themes can be a tip-off. If a dream has medical imagery, such as the presence of a doctor or a drugstore, it makes sense to look at it more closely for evidence of that intuitive, sixth sense at work with some very practical guidance.

Often dreams that offer health warnings point to the detrimental effects of activities of the waking life. Oftentimes dreams that are set in the dining room or kitchen hint at a problem in diet. Vehicles, especially cars, are sometimes symbolic of the physical body.

Certain themes in the plot of a dream may refer to conditions of the body—for example, getting caught in a long highway backup may be indicative of intestinal blockage, or running out of money while shopping might symbolize the depletion of your physical energy. The body may warn about the effects of smoking cigarettes through a dream in which the breath is being restricted.

Not only do dreams offer sixth sense insight into our physical health and relationships with others; they also offer a way to know ourselves better. But what happens when we are unable to understand their meaning or even remember them in the first place? Is the impact of the sixth sense in sleep lost? By no means. We must simply look to the second avenue for this intuitive, nightly wisdom.

THE SIXTH SENSE IN THE HYPNAGOGIC STATE

There are two periods each night of what is sometimes called "half sleep" because we have a foot in each of two worlds—one in waking life and one in the domain of sleep. The first period happens as we are falling asleep. That middle ground as we drift off is called the hypnagogic state. A second period is psychologically very similar, but if refers to those moments when we are coming out of the sleep world and back into waking consciousness. Those few seconds or minutes have been labeled the hypnopompic state. However, in modern language the technical reference gets blurred (as we will let it do here in this chapter), and both periods of half-sleep are referred to as the hypnagogic state.

These special periods present a rather unique opportunity in consciousness each day. The mind retains a portion of its wakeful, analytical awareness, while simultaneously there are images and feelings that flow in naturally when the physical senses have been diminished. It is as if we are getting a few moments of the best of both worlds. The conscious mind is fleetingly able to tap into the resources of the unconscious mind.

Sometimes this all may seem too obscure and delicate to make practical, but it is worth continuing to pay attention to and to explore this fascinating way in which the sixth sense can shine through. The key is to make it a habit to notice what comes from these half sleep periods. Be patient with the fact that there will be days when you catch nothing or days when whatever you do remember doesn't seem to make such sense. Cayce emphasized that there will be instances—maybe only occasional—in which significant insights from the soul *can* spring forth.

Here is one way to approach the nurturance of these special periods. Try to wake up gently and naturally, rather than abruptly from a buzzing alarm. If an alarm is necessary, try one with the radio station playing classical music or soft jazz. As you begin to be aware of yourself in the bed, pay attention to how you feel or any imagery that is present. If it seems like you have been in a dream, see if you can let the dream or its feelings continue for just another minute or two.

Lie there in bed and let random impressions come into your attention. Occasionally you may seem to drift back into a state in which spontaneous, nonlogical thoughts, ideas, and imagery come to mind. Then, once you begin to sense that you really are more awake than asleep, start to notice your mood, thoughts, and ideas. Simply pay attention to any new ideas or impressions the night has left with you. Do you have any fresh insight about your life? You don't need to know where it came from or how you came up with that insight. Just be open and receptive to what your sixth sense has been working on while you were sleeping and is now ready to offer you. And make it a habit to record these feelings, thoughts, and insights in a journal, much as you would your dreams. (You can even use the same journal book for both.)

An Experiment with Your Sixth Sense in Sleep

To make this even more practical, consider how you can

use your dreams and the hypnagogic state as sources of guidance about specific issues in your life. Allow your sixth sense in sleep to ponder a question that your conscious mind has been struggling with. It might be a health concern, a relationship problem, or the need for spiritual guidance.

It will probably help this experiment if you will write the problem or question on paper just before you go to sleep. As you drift off, keep thinking about the question and your desire for an answer that night. Take care not to worry endlessly about the situation or it may keep you awake, thus defeating the purpose. Instead, calmly consider the problem or question, and ask your deeper mind to work on it during the night.

When you awake the next morning, lie still for a few minutes. See if you drift back into the half-sleep state. Do any hypnagogic images, thoughts, or impressions come up? Do you have any strong feelings just beneath the surface? Then, when you are fully awake, spend a minute or two before you get out of bed recalling any dreams you may have had that night. Be alert to recall both the dream storyline and any emotions that were part of the dream.

Finally, before you get out of bed, notice your mood, thoughts, and ideas. How has the night's sleep influenced you? Turn your attention to your question or problem, and think about it for a moment. Does any new angle on the issue arise? From among all these bits and pieces of information that have been stimulated by sleep, what clues do you get about an answer to your problem?

Once you are up, spend some time recording in your journal the impressions, images, and insights you've had. Some mornings you may not have much to write. You may not have been able to remember a dream or catch a hypnagogic image. That's OK. Don't be discouraged. Simply record anything you do remember or any creative thought you found yourself having that morning when you thought once again about your question or issue.

On other days the experiment may seem more fruitful. You might have a page full of hypnagogic images to record, plus another couple of pages of dreams. You might have several valuable insights about your issue or perhaps even a full-blown solution to the problem!

And give yourself a little time before deciding if the night's effort paid dividends or not. Sometimes you see no immediate relationship between your stated problem and the images that came in the hypnagogic state or the dream you remembered. But during the course of the day, something may happen to you that will suddenly awaken an insight into the meaning of what was presented to you from the sixth sense in sleep.

Finding answers through our unconscious mind and sixth sense is not always easy. It can take practice and great trust in your dreams and the creative imagery that arises from half-sleep. The more you work with your sixth sense in sleep, the more you will understand how it communicates with your conscious mind and can be a tool for your spiritual development.

A MODERN DAY SUCCESS WITH THIS POSITIVE HABIT

Alisa, a teacher from southern California, spent a considerable amount of time at the beach as she was growing up and almost as much on into her adult life. Her hair was dark and she naturally had a fairly dark complexion that tanned easily and rarely burned.

As a teenager at the beach, Alisa almost never wore sunscreen, but instead slathered tanning oil on her body when she laid out in the sun. "It just wasn't something we worried about, my girlfriends and I. It was almost a competition to see who could get the darkest."

By her thirties, Alisa loved the beach no less, and her skin showed it in the form of tiny wrinkles. By now, Alisa had taken up the habit of wearing sunscreen when she would go out for extended periods of time. "By the time I was thirty, though, the damage had been done to my skin. I was more wrinkled than maybe I should have been. But I liked being tan, it just made me look healthy."

In her mid-thirties, Alisa was at a routine physical when a nurse noticed a small raised green patch on the back of her upper arm. Alisa had to strain her neck to even see it, but sure enough, it was there. "My first reaction was to kind of dismiss it, but I tend to do that with things I don't particularly want to deal with. I was not even interested in getting it checked out right away. Frankly, I thought if I ignored it, it would go away."

The doctor did not share her wait-and-see attitude; he decided it warranted some tests. Alisa was sent to a specialist who would run the tests necessary to determine if it was melanoma.

"When the doctor said 'melanoma,' I kind of panicked. I didn't know much about skin cancer, but I did know melanoma was deadly. It sounds ignorant, but since I almost never had a sunburn, I didn't think I was at risk for skin cancer."

Too nervous to wait for the results of the medical test to come back, Alisa decided to try to get her own intuition about the situation. She knew from experience how the sixth sense in sleep could work, and she had used it with some success earlier. But she was a little out of practice. But feeling sure that the wisdom of her body knew if the suspicious spot on her skin was cancer, she believed that somehow she could tap into that knowledge. The night before Alisa's tests were to be done, she scribbled out a question on a napkin. "Do I have skin cancer?" Putting the napkin under her pillow, she slipped into sleep, repeating the question to herself.

Later she recalled some anxiety about whether her dreams would be the source of a reliable answer. "When I try to dream about something really important, I end up having nightmares about the worst possible scenario. In the morning I am left trying to decide whether it was a psychic experience or my mind going crazy. I half expected to have a dream about a slow death from the cancer and wake up terrified."

Alisa's answer that night came, however, not as a dream but instead as hypnagogic images she caught as she awakened.

"I could feel myself waking up, but my eyes were still closed. Then it seemed as if my eyes opened on their own. I didn't open them; they just flew open. When they did, it was like I saw my eyelids flip up like two great big shutters. The insides were blue. On one eyelid there was the letter 'N' and on the other the letter 'O' both in white. Then I stopped being able to see the letters and the room came into focus. It was very quick, like one fluid movement. I just knew immediately what this meant, that my deeper mind was speaking right to me. It was wonderful. And I had such a feeling of relief about me. I almost didn't want to go have the tests done because I just knew the answer already."

Alisa did, however, go to the doctor and had a series of tests. The patch on her skin was not cancerous. She had it removed anyway, as the doctor suggested. He warned her to pay careful attention to anything new on her skin since she had already done significant damage and was not in the clear for skin cancer. Alisa took the doctor's advice very seriously and is now an avid user of sunscreen—*and* an avid user of her sixth sense in sleep for other concerns as they arise.

A Story from the Cayce Archives

The Blumenthals are probably the finest example of a family getting guidance from their personal dreams, enhanced by the interpretive insights of Edgar Cayce. The Blumenthal brothers—Morton and Edwin—were very successful stockbrokers, both in their twenties, when they met Cayce. Largely because of their enthusiasm and financial support, Cayce and his family moved to Virginia Beach, with the hope of founding a clinic or hospital that would use natural healing methods.

The Blumenthals' deep involvement in the business side of Cayce's work carried over into their personal lives. Both brothers received a vast number of readings in the seven years they were a key part of Cayce's inner circle of helpers. Morton got 468 personal readings; Edwin, 132. Many of those readings focused on dream interpretation. Morton's wife Adeline was also a frequent recipient of dream interpretation guidance from Cayce. All told, Morton had 540 of his dreams interpreted by Cayce; Adeline, 142; Edwin, 115; and Edwin's wife another 15 dreams. It's an extraordinary case study of a dreaming family and what they learned about the sixth sense in sleep.

Morton in particular had the frequent experiences at night with his sixth sense. His innate intuition would often express itself not so much as a complicated dream which needed interpretation but instead as simply a "voice," as he called it. The "voice" would offer a message that often had direct advice about some problem or issue from waking life. However, in other instances, that sixth sense presented its wisdom via a dream; and Cayce had deep insight into the meaning or message of those dream experiences.

Many of the dream interpretations by Cayce appear to have followed one of the three methods outlined in the three-method dream interpreter strategy already outlined in this chapter. No doubt, Morton, Adeline, and Edwin became avid interpreters of their own dreams, and we can expect that following Cayce's deciphering strategies they probably used methods such as this series of three questions:

- How am I changed from having gone through this dream?
- How has this dream come to balance or compensate for some extreme in my life?
- What could this dream be telling me about my physical body?

Illustrating the first method, Morton once dreamed that he was talking with a friend and told that person that he was giving all his profits from land investments to a certain charitable cause. In response Morton received considerable criticism and ridicule in the dream. Edwin then appeared in the dream and found fault with Morton for having been so disclosing about his intentions. At first Morton claimed that he couldn't help it, but then realized that it would have been best if he had not said these things to his friend. Then Morton woke up. (900-376)

Although being able to get Cayce's interpretation was useful, Morton could see the meaning of the dream, simply by applying the first option among the three methods. How had he been changed merely by having gone through this experience? His attitude and understanding about "good works" had been altered. He now realized that it's inappropriate to brag about his good intentions. Cayce's perspective said as much to him: " . . . let not thy good be evil spoken of through any effort of thine self to appear above the ordinary individual. Let rather what would be said, concerning good deeds done from any source, come from others rather than from self."

Adeline had a dream that fits nicely into the category of balancing or compensating. She was twenty-one at the time, recently married to Morton and very interested in starting a family. She was also concerned about looking good and maintaining her health. Diet had become a big issue for her. One dream came right at a time when she had rigorously (and rather abruptly) removed all sugar and sweets from her daily diet. This rather bizarre dream—

hardly what she was actually doing in waking life—left her discouraged. She was sitting at a table eating—but more than eating, she was "packing it in." As she told the dream to Cayce, "There was chocolate cake, coconut cake, and all kinds of sweets and goodies" and she just had a great time eating it all up. (136-20)

In fact, her dream behavior *was* extreme—even the *opposite* extreme from what she was doing in waking life. Her new, daily approach had been absolutely no sweets, and here in the dream she is overindulging. But the very fact that the dream behavior was so extreme should have tipped her off to its meaning. It is a compensatory dream that has come to balance her. As Cayce put it: "The entity recognizes in this the opposite from that being enacted in the daily life . . . Then eat more sweets, see? Not in excess, in moderation . . . " To her body and its consciousness, Adeline had gone to an extreme, and balance would be reestablished only by finding a modest way to include a few sweets.

Just a few weeks later she brought another dream to Cayce for advice. The meaning of this one is revealed by the third interpretation method: looking for guidance about the physical body. Here the tip-off was the way in which a part of her body played a key role in the dream story. "I was going to swim from a rickety platform—very unsubstantial in its structure. As I jumped in or tried to dive in, I made a belly whapper—i.e., landed on my stomach—it hurt." (136-21) Her stomach (or belly region) is a central focus in the dream. Cayce's interpretation for Adeline concerned her interest in starting a family and the condition of her health at the time. Her body was not prepared for the pregnancy she hoped for. Like the rickety platform, it wasn't very stable. And if she attempted to jump into pregnancy right away, she was liable to get hurt. The warning dream seems to have played itself out because just a few months later she got pregnant but then miscarried. Happily, about a year and a half later she had a successful pregnancy, with Morton and her becoming parents of a son. Not surprisingly, dream study was an important part of their marriage during the pregnancy and as new parents— with dozens of dream interpretations by Cayce about those opportunities and challenges.

APPLYING THIS POSITIVE HABIT TO YOUR LIFE

Each day for a week try to be particularly sensitive to the inner resource of your intuition as you are sleeping. At night when you get ready for bed, take a moment to remember that your soul mind will be active throughout the night, available and willing to consider whatever issues have challenged or troubled you during the daytime. For some of the evenings during this week, you might even want to select a specific difficulty and invite your sixth sense to be working on it while you sleep.

Then, for each morning of this week, be sure to take just a couple of extra minutes in bed when you wake up. Let yourself stay in the hypnagogic state for just a little while. Pay attention to your feelings and your mood after having been asleep all those hours. Try to see beyond whether or not you are excited about the day ahead. Instead, pay attention to impressions or insights that might come into consciousness—the product of your sixth sense's efforts during the night. And, of course, be especially alert during this experimental week to dreams that you may recall. Sometimes they are the very best example of your sixth sense and its capacity to provide you with help for staying centered—spiritually, mentally, and physically.

calories fat content diet regular exercise healthy lifestyle fitness

Keeping Daily Rhythms Keeping Daily Rhythms

Positive
Habit
#10

Keeping Daily Rhythms

The world in which most of us live is fast-paced and hectic. Too easily a day can become disjointed, and we can be left feeling as if we are controlled by circumstances beyond our reach. Sometimes it is the mere unpredictability of a day which can throw us off kilter, disorient us, and leave our energies drained.

But then there are days when we find a rhythm, when we hit our stride. An inner orderliness can allow us to meet the outer world—with all its uncertainty and stress—and still have plenty of energy and vitality. The positive habit of finding and keeping a daily rhythm allows us to handle uncertainty with grace, and thus we can become more spiritually centered.

The inner orderliness that comes from daily rhythms begins with the positive use of the free will. What you will to do, and then follow through and actually do, in turn gives you force. In other words, as you use free will to initiate chosen activities in your day, you'll gain energy rather than be depleted of it.

Probably we have all experienced this principle at work in our lives, whether or not we were conscious of it. When you choose to do something and really want to do it, the very activity can be energizing. In contrast, when you feel like circumstances force you to do things and you begrudgingly comply, the likely result is fatigue.

Of course, we can hardly expect lifestyles that permit us to do what we want all day long. Responsibilities and demands are a large part of life. Nevertheless, the creative use of our free will can give us control, even when we are faced with that which we must do. And how do we get ourselves organized and focused enough to follow that strategy? The secret is the use of personal rhythms.

By creating the positive habit of personal rhythms during the day, we can retain a sense of centeredness; and it is through free will that we create and retain these rhythms. Rhythms, or cycles, are dependable patterns in life. They are ever present and a reminder that we live in an orderly universe.

The so-called "circadian rhythm" of a daily twenty-four-hour cycle is one example. The rhythms of day impact us both biologically and psychologically. Medical research has shown that the body is like a highly sensitive clock that moves through distinct states in the course of one day. If you observe yourself carefully, you'll probably notice how you follow reliable patterns. There are peaks and valleys to your alertness, creativity, energy level, and many other factors. The differences from person to person can be as opposite as night and day; however, for each individual, consistent rhythms can usually be identified.

Holistic healing practices often come in the form of rhythms and cycles. Many packs, poultices, and herbal tonics are most effective when used in a rhythmic pattern. An "on" then "off" sequence of application—that is, use for several consecutive days and then nonuse for several days—has an underlying rationale. This rhythmic, cyclical approach to healing creates days of nontreatment in which the body can integrate the effects of treatment and then respond with its own self-healing resources.

The body also responds best to exercise when done in a

rhythmic cycle. For example, Cayce suggests that there is a basic tendency in most bodies for greater blood circulation and muscular activity in the upper body during the day and for the trunk and lower body in the evening. Tying this into patterns of physical exercise, we have a natural rhythm for calisthenics or stretching exercises: upper body in the morning, lower in the evening.

Even though natural patterns of timing are all around us and within us, we tend to be oblivious of these patterns. Why? In part, modern technology has largely allowed us to insulate ourselves from the dependency on natural rhythms. Centuries ago, people were more in touch with fundamental cycles. Without electricity, central heating, and fresh fruits and vegetables being shipped in from the corners of the world, there was an awareness of and dependency on the cycles of the weather, nature, and their own bodies.

Something deep within us suffers as a result of all the conveniences that technology has produced. It is a profound challenge in the modern world to feel and understand natural cycles. Where do we begin? The first step is to recognize and understand the patterns of the body. We can start by simply being aware of the ebb and flow of feelings and energy. This leads to greater awareness of the cyclic nature of life, and we begin to feel more at home on the earth and in our bodies. Next, we can begin to *create* rhythms—consciously—for ourselves. Making that work a positive habit can go a long way toward maintaining a sense of control and centeredness in the midst of a hectic or disjointed day.

Of course, there is no single rhythmic pattern that works for everyone. Attention to one's own natural cycles is crucial. However, consider starting with a straightforward principle and adapting its essential themes to your own life. The folk adage recommends, "After breakfast work a while, after lunch rest a while, after supper walk a mile."

It's catchy because it rhymes. But it's practical and provides an easy way to create rhythm in one's day.

The formula—which can eventually become an important, positive habit—is something that is relatively easy to try. You can do it literally or, as we'll see, by personally adjusting its essential themes. It's a matter of experimenting with small investments of energy, strategically timed to create a rhythmic orderliness to your day. By using your free will and choosing to follow even the most simple rhythm, you're likely to reap big rewards.

Let's look carefully at each aspect of this three-part formula. Each portion can be adapted to fit your own lifestyle. One person may try to apply the formula exactly as it's stated, while another person will redesign the activities somewhat.

After breakfast work a while.   The question here concerns the meaning of "work." Does it mean physical labor, such as raking leaves or cleaning the house? Or does it mean mental work, such as creating a detailed report or balancing the checkbook? The best interpretation of this folk wisdom is a broad one. "Work a while" can mean an activity done not as idle routine or boring drudgery, but instead *with consciousness*—with attention, creativity, and purpose.

For many of us working a while in the morning is not a matter of choice. "If I don't work a while after breakfast, I'll lose my job!" But even with the structure of job duties, can you designate some type of work task to be done every morning with special attention, care, and creativity? That is creating a rhythm.

For a person who spends the morning at home, there is more room for flexibility in picking a work activity. You may have the choice of doing physical work or mental work. It might be a household task. It might be working on a relationship, such as calling a friend or writing a letter. It might be study or creative writing.

After lunch, rest a while. In many cultures resting after lunch is commonplace. An actual nap may or may not be possible for you. But the goal is to look for some kind of afternoon routine that has recuperative qualities. Most office and production line workers are entitled to an afternoon break of ten or fifteen minutes, although the time sometimes isn't used in a truly restful way. For a hurried parent at home, "rest a while" might mean a ten-minute break to sit and have tea or read. For a busy executive, it could be holding all calls for five minutes and reading the newspaper or stretching the back. Even for a person who cannot stop his or her responsibilities in the afternoon, perhaps a minute or two could be spent in deep breathing at about the same time each day in the afternoon.

After supper walk a mile. Modern day health professionals can testify to the benefits of exercise. If there are no significant obstacles, consider taking this part of the adage literally. However, in your life situation walking may or may not be possible in the evenings. A physical handicap or a neighborhood where walking in the evening is unsafe could make a literal interpretation impossible. Perhaps a good substitute could be weeding the garden for a while or doing yoga in the living room after your meal has had time to digest.

If for whatever reason evening physical activity is impossible, you can still create a version of this positive habit. Instead of some form of exercise, you could designate some other creative form of activity "after supper." Maybe it will be family discussion or a game. Or perhaps it will be some type of outreach to others, such as phoning a friend or writing a letter. The point is to create the reliable rhythm to your day.

A STORY FROM THE CAYCE ARCHIVES

Marla was desperate. She had become accustomed to

this feeling because she had considered herself very ill for a long time, and in those twenty years she felt that no doctor had offered any really useful advice. She always felt mentally exhausted, and most days she felt physically depleted, as well. On those rare "good days" she could make it to the grocery or to yet another disappointing doctor's appointment, but inevitably she would end up having to go to bed early.

On top of her general fatigue and her inflamed intestinal track, Marla feared that she had a mental disorder. The symptoms were feeling extremely tense and nervous most of the time. Everyone in her family there in Texas was worried about her, but the doctors just seemed to think that she needed more rest in the day and better sleep at night.

From a friend she learned about a new biography entitled *There Is a River* and quickly got a copy of the book so she could read about this man who was being touted as the source of healing miracles. By the time she wrote to him, she wasn't the only one seeking this kind of help for a health emergency. November 1943 was a very demanding time for Edgar Cayce. His fame had rapidly spread because of not one but two publications about his work. The demand for his assistance was almost overwhelming. In the midst of this period, he received Marla's letter. It began: "If I have addressed this letter to the wrong party won't you be good enough to pass it along to the proper person?" Apparently she wasn't sure that Mr. Cayce was really the source of answers that she had hoped for, but she continued: "I have just learned through reading some of your literature that there is a hospital—an Edgar Cayce hospital—in Virginia Beach. I have been terribly ill for the last twenty years and no doctor has been able to find my trouble or help me."

Even though she had misunderstood and there was no longer a Cayce hospital facility, nevertheless, a health diagnosis reading was arranged for her in January 1944.

Among her questions to be answered in the reading were:
- What causes this terrible tiredness of my mind and body, and lack of strength? What can be done to cure it?
- Do I have a mental disorder? If so, what is it and how can it be cured?
- I am extremely tense and nervous most of the time—what can be done for this?

While in the unconscious state from which he dispensed clairvoyant medical advice, Cayce began, "As we find, there are disturbances with this body. These are primarily the effect of a despondency and a nervous shock to the whole system . . . These as we find, are the basis or sources of the tiredness, the restlessness, the insomnia at times, the headaches, the general drain on the system . . . " Then, he added an emphatic "No!" when asked if she had a mental disorder.

Cayce's prescription to counteract the condition began with improvements in lifestyle. "First, here, begin with the mental attitude. For here there must be more purposefulness, more general planning in the hopes and desires of the mental and physical body. The spirit is willing, the flesh has proven weak."

By focusing the issue largely as a matter of free will, he emphasized that the stimulus for healing was within her power. It would not be easy to create new patterns for living, but they were likely to be more crucial to a cure than any tonic or medicine. He continued, "Do take plenty of time for rest. Do take time for plenty of definite labors . . . take time to work, to think, to make contacts for a social life and for recreation. This old adage might well apply: After breakfast, work a while, after lunch rest a while, after dinner walk a mile. This as a recreation may be a helpful, balanced experience for this life." (3624-1)

The reading went on to suggest some physical procedures as well, such as osteopathic adjustments. But the essence of Cayce's advice was the development of a positive habit for building a rhythmic pattern into her lifestyle. Marla discovered, as any of us might, however, that creating new patterns with the force of free will isn't easy. There are always distractions and important events to take our attention elsewhere. In her case, it was a crisis with her son.

Writing to Cayce several months later, she confirmed that he had accurately described her frame of mind. "I do not know as to the physical part (as I honestly could not tell what was wrong with me) but the mental condition or attitude was described accurately." However, the duties of being a supportive mother had kept her from making progress on the new daily rhythm that Cayce had advocated. She admitted in her follow-up letter, "I apologize for waiting so long to write after the reading, but the fact is my son had arrived home from Marine boot-training at San Diego the night before I received the reading in a serious condition with rheumatic fever and pneumonia. He is now in the Naval Hospital in New Orleans and will be there for some time. I have been so disturbed, and my routine of living so disrupted . . . "

Sadly, there is no further correspondence from Marla; and Cayce himself stopped giving readings just a few months later because of his own illness that led to his death. Nevertheless, this story from the Cayce archival files illustrates Cayce's position that sometimes the things that ail us can best be addressed from a psychological perspective, including the use of our free will to start building some new lifestyle patterns—ones that will invite a greater sense of spiritual centeredness and mastery of our affairs.

A MODERN DAY SUCCESS WITH THIS POSITIVE HABIT

In November of 1998, Anita retired from her profession in the medical field in the hopes of bringing more balance into her life. "The demands of my career had left me burned out from sixty-hour work weeks and the stress resulting from the downsizing, merging, and changes that resulted from the influx of managed care. Now, rather than having a list of things that had to get done today, or more like yesterday, I could have a list of things I needed and wanted to do for the week."

But coming out of a world of many demands and moving directly into one with very few expectations can create a confusing transition period. Anita found herself in need of a life pattern in her newly unstructured lifestyle. When someone spends years operating at a hurried pace, it can be quite a shock to try to operate at a more mellow cadence.

With the same efficiency for which she was known in the office, Anita began to create structure in her life that allowed for downtime as well as productivity. At the same time, she had the opportunity to develop her spiritual life and take care of her health. "At home I diligently set about constructing a chart for myself to identify and record my progress at incorporating several activities into my daily schedule. I adapted Cayce's adage, 'After breakfast work a while, after lunch rest a while, and after dinner walk a mile' to my own physical energy pattern which had only recently come into my awareness. By the third week my energy level had risen a noticeable amount and my sleep had improved even more."

Anita was very satisfied with her new rhythmic lifestyle, but after a month of keeping this daily rhythm a new challenge arose. She was selected to work parttime in her community for the nationwide Census 2000, a job for which she had applied a year earlier but then assumed wasn't going to come through. The responsibilities of the new job changed the way Anita structured her day, and it required a spiritual centeredness to stay committed to the positive habit she had been working on developing. Her own belief system was that "it takes twenty-one days to form (or break) a habit; and, sure enough, her month of experience with the new, positive habit pattern was strong enough to survive the fresh demands on her daily schedule.

"Because I had formed the habit of accounting to myself on a daily basis for keeping my daily rhythms, I was able to remain quite in balance through this mild upheaval in my life. I may have missed a meditation on a couple of days, or missed relaxing on a night or two. But because I accounted to myself every day, I soon became aware of the imbalance and got back on track much sooner than if I had not been paying attention to my body's rhythms."

Ten months later the job with Census 2000 was over, and Anita returned to her previous lifestyle. She attributed her successful adaptation of the switches in activity level to the sense of rhythm she was able to maintain over those months. She had long ago discovered that it wasn't necessary to keep a daily record of her compliance with the positive habits.

"It has been months now since I stopped charting my activities on a daily basis, but the habit is now ingrained. My consciousness is permanently raised, so that I almost daily ask myself the following questions: What physical activity have I done today? What have I done for relaxation? Have I meditated or spent time alone? How is my energy and sleep? Am I feeling in control, or are outside influences taking over?"

The simple use of creating daily rhythms changed Anita's life significantly. She became better able to deal with changes life brought her way—even unexpected opportunities that at one time in her life might have more easily caused her to get life out of balance. Keeping daily rhythms grounded her and kept chaos at bay. Overall the experience of rhythms was one of the most positive of Anita's life.

APPLYING THIS POSITIVE HABIT TO YOUR LIFE

Consider how your own life could benefit from the positive habit of a daily rhythm. Remember the principle that what you choose to do and then follow through on can actually give you energy, rather than deplete it.

Perhaps the adage recommended frequently by Cayce will work for you. "After breakfast work a while." That is, find a way to be creative or productive for a focused time in the morning. Maybe it's a matter of just a little extra attention to the tasks you are already obligated to do. Or perhaps your lifestyle affords a little more freedom from obligations, and you can choose daily what you'd like to do in the morning that seems productive and creative.

Then, "after lunch rest a while." Look for a way to have at least a few minutes for rest, relaxation, or rejuvenation in the early part of the afternoon. It might not take the same form every day, but can you find a way to make something replenishing a positive habit at this time each day?

Finally, "after dinner walk a mile." If it's not actually walking, is there some other type of physical exercise that allows you purposefully to move the limbs of your body in the early evening—perhaps some stretch? Or, if you are just not an evening exercise enthusiast, what other kind of positive, creative pattern could you build into your lifestyle for early evenings?

Once you have a plan for how to adapt this Cayce recommendation to your own life, then make a commitment to try it for at least a week. Perhaps you'll begin to notice some changes in various aspects of your life—your feeling of centeredness, your energy level, or your sense of control over your life. You may also find that the more days you try this positive habit, the easier it becomes to keep it up.

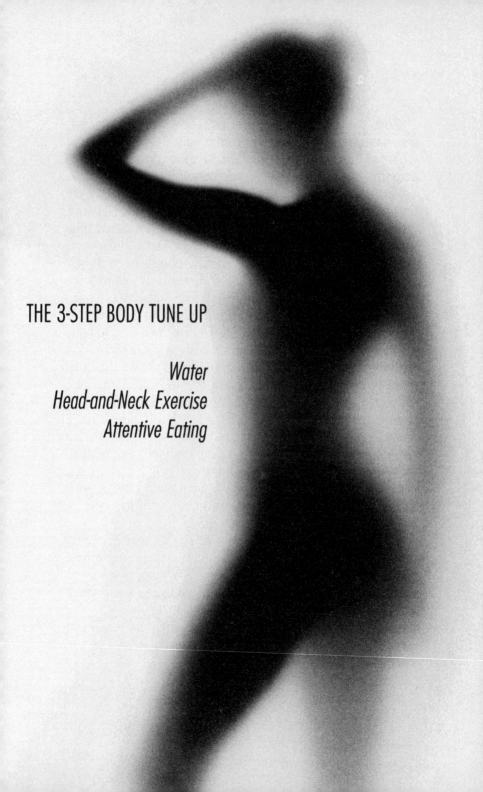

THE 3-STEP BODY TUNE UP

Water
Head-and-Neck Exercise
Attentive Eating

Positive
Habit
#11

Three-Step Body Tuneup

All around us are signs of the physical fitness craze. Joggers, bran cereals, and exercise spas, just to name a few. Advertisements in magazines and on television would have us believe that almost everyone is doing it.

But are these apparent signs an accurate picture of what's going on in most people's lives? Just how seriously do we actually take our health? If we look carefully at our lives, most of us aren't satisfied with the amount of time and energy we commit to maintaining physical well-being. Most likely, there are many days when we find ourselves simply too tired to give our bodies the attention they deserve.

Most of us understand the need to take care of ourselves physically. We want to live our lives free of illness, to maintain a healthy weight, and keep up the natural energy that comes from good care of the body. But besides those obvious physical benefits, a strong body also affects the health of our spiritual lives. Any positive health habits we can maintain are also likely to have a big impact on how we stay spiritually connected.

The key to understanding why positive health habits impact our spiritual centeredness lies in how we view the body itself. When we try to step back and get the big picture of ourselves—that is, as beings of the spirit and not limited by the material world—it can be tempting to think of the physical body as merely something we own and occupy temporarily, much like we own a car for a few years. But that's really dualistic thinking. It splits the body from the mind (and spirit) in a way that makes authentic wholeness hard to imagine. Another point of view would be to see the body as an expression of the invisible sides of ourselves, such as mind and spirit. The body is part and parcel of the deeper and unseen aspects of who we know ourselves to be. And if that's the case, then anything that we do to revitalize and enhance the body will have a beneficial effect on the mind and spirit, too.

You're probably the sort of person who would like to be doing more to keep your body in the best condition, but you rarely seem to get around to acting on that good intention quite as fully as you'd like. Edgar Cayce's health advice to thousands of people includes many tips that can be incorporated in your lifestyle without huge investments of time and energy. This chapter focuses on three simple methods to keep your body tuned—or, as Cayce more often put it "attuned." These positive habits, each of which requires only a minimal amount of time, can result in some very significant differences.

Cayce gave specific health readings for men and women with particular ailments, but he also presented general guidelines for maintaining a healthy body, ideas that are applicable to anyone wishing to improve his or her health. What we are calling here the "three-step body tuneup" focuses on a manageable number of those basic guidelines. The goals of each one is to enhance energy, decrease stress, and increase total awareness of the body.

Of course, there are no shortcuts to good health. Vitality and wellness are the products of established lifestyle patterns that promote the best potentials within our bodies. Good health is not something that can be achieved from a quick physical tuneup. Rather, the tuneup is a *starting* point, a way to focus on the habits that will ensure a healthy body. Incorporate the body tuneup into your current health regime; make it part of your daily routine.

Drink plenty of water.

Most people either forget to drink sufficient amounts of water or they underestimate just how much water they need for optimal health. Adequate consumption of water is probably the most basic "dietary" principle. It impacts the way the body functions in all stages of the digestion process.

Water intake influences assimilations. Although it's certainly correct to be concerned about what we eat—for nutritious foods, properly assimilated, are the building blocks of a healthy body—good eliminations are just as important. In fact, in one Cayce reading we find a remarkable promise about *longevity* if these two processes are maintained normally. As Cayce put it: " . . . for would the assimilations and the eliminations be kept nearer *normal* in the human family, the days might be extended to whatever period as was so desired; for the system is builded by the assimilations of that it takes within, and is able to bring resuscitations so long as the eliminations do not hinder." (311-4)

Sufficient water intake is one key to good eliminations, and that means water itself and not merely juices, milk, or other liquids that contain water. No doubt they have a place in a balanced diet, but the emphasis should be on drinking simply water. As Cayce put it to someone who asked whether or not he was drinking enough water and juice to keep the kidneys and colon flushed, "Drink *water* rather than so much juices . . . Not sufficient water taken!" (1703-2)

The question, of course, is how much water to drink each day. The answer is somewhat different for each person. In Cayce's health recommendations to various people—each with a unique body and unique needs—the answer ranged from a low of "three to four glasses daily" for one person to a high of "six to ten *pints*" for someone else. The most frequent recommendation was six to eight *glasses* daily. That matches well the advice given by most contemporary nutritionists and doctors.

Interestingly, there were also recommendations about *how* to drink the water and when to do so. Perhaps it sounds funny that someone would try to coach us on how to drink a glass of water, but Cayce had some novel ideas on this issue. For example, he sometimes told people that some of their water drinking should include "chewing" the water slightly—that is allowing saliva to mix with the water before swallowing it. As he put it to one man, "Even . . . water should be *chewed* two to three times before taken into the stomach itself, for this makes for the proper assimilation of the lacteal activity in the system . . . " (808-3) And that same man was further instructed to avoid using water (or any liquid) as a way of washing down his food. "Bolting food or swallowing it by the use of liquids produces more colds than *any one* activity of a diet!" In other words, let the food be ingested and then in the stomach digested without interference from heavy water drinking.

You may not find it easy to get your entire allotment of water in a day. For that reason, you might want to start your day off with a glass of water in the morning, as you first wake up. Spaced between breakfast and lunch drink two glasses. Have three more glasses spaced through the hours of the afternoon, and another two glasses in the evening.

Maybe it sounds excessive. You may find yourself wondering, "How can I ever remember to refill my glass so many times?" But with practice it becomes a positive habit. It will become automatic, and you'll wonder how you previously survived without plenty of water!

SEEKING INFORMATION ON

holistic health, spirituality, dreams, intuition or ancient civilizations?

Call 1-800-723-1112, visit our Web site, or mail in this postage-paid card for a FREE catalog of books and membership information.

Name: _____

Address: _____

City: _____

State/Province: _____

Postal/Zip Code: _____ Country: _____

Association for Research and Enlightenment, Inc.
215 67th Street
Virginia Beach, VA 23451-2061

For faster service, call 1-800-723-1112.
www.edgarcayce.org

PBIN

Stretch the head and neck.

Exercise is an important part of any body tuneup program, but what kind of regimen works best? Walking and stretching were the two most frequently mentioned approaches by Cayce. Of the two, stretching is probably the most universally accepted positive habit to cultivate. Even people who find walking difficult—that is, because of safety reasons or because of a physical handicap—can usually find some sort of stretching exercise that is helpful. Here's a typical piece of advice from Cayce to one person who asked for health information. Notice that a distinction is made between stretching and straining. "The exercise that we would follow for this body would be the stretching much in the manner as the exercise of the cat or the panther, or that type of activity; stretching the muscular forces, not as strains but as to cause the tendons and muscles to be put into position for the formation of strength-building to the body." (4003-1)

Probably the one stretching exercise that was mentioned by Cayce more often than any other was a series of head-and-neck movements. This exercise was described in slightly different ways in various readings, but in each case the basic elements are identical. As Cayce put it to one sixty-five-year-old man, emphasizing at the end just how important it is to make this discipline into a positive habit, "Sitting erect bend the head forward three times at least, then back as far as it may be bent three times, to the right side three times; then to the left side three times. Then circle the head and neck to the right three times, then to the left three times. Be consistent with this though, not just doing it occasionally." (5404-1)

What benefits are promised from this stretching exercise? Frequently it was recommended for improvements in the sensory organs, especially for better eyesight. Any positive effects of this sort would likely take far longer than just a week or even a month. But a more immediate centering and health-promoting effect might come, especially in relation to stress.

Most of us have noticed that tension is often stored by our bodies in the neck and shoulder areas. This tendency may be even more pronounced in today's world which has even more sedentary desk jobs than in Cayce's era of the 1920s, '30s, and '40s. Both osteopaths and chiropractors have noted that muscular tension and resultant misalignments in the neck area can, in turn, produce other problems lower in the spinal column and in the body as a whole. Relaxation for the neck and shoulder muscles may well be one key to overall health. The secret to effective application of this positive habit is threefold:

1) Do it slowly. The basic movements can potentially be completed in a minute or less, but that's rushing it. When you hurry the movements, they actually may be counterproductive, either causing muscles to be strained or creating new tension. Take two to three minutes to complete all the steps. That requires a deliberate motion that takes the time to feel the gentle stretching effect.

2) Do it consistently. To develop the positive habit, complete the exercise at least once daily. You may even want to try it several times a day! As Cayce put it to one forty-four-year-old man, "Also we would take the head-and-neck exercise consistently; not just take it one day and forget it the next, or take it once a week or three to four times a week and leave off, but take it morning and evening—two to three minutes." (1564-2)

3) Do it purposefully. As you complete the motions, remember why you are doing it. Think relaxation. Imagine your body becoming more healthy so that your life can be more centered—spiritually, mentally, and physically.

Eat consciously and with a thankful attitude.

Seventy years ago Cayce asserted that our attitudes play an important role in determining our health. And today, the expanding research field of medicine called psycho-neuroimmunology is establishing the relationship between the mental states and the capacity of the body to ward off illness. Psychoneuroimmunology studies the effect of the mind (psycho) and the nervous system (neuro) on the immune system (immunology). Research in the last fifteen years has shown that the state of a person's emotional wellness directly affects his or her physical well-being. Stress, depression, and anxiety impair the immune system, while happiness, appreciation, and inspiration strengthen it.

Research like this gives us further evidence into the power of the mind. Perhaps the simplest place in your life to start experimenting with this principle is your mental state while you are eating. It's easy to take eating for granted—not just *what* you eat but *how* you do so. As noted earlier, bolting down our food is not a good idea, but we're encouraged to do more than just eat slowly. For one thing, it's best to avoid eating when you are in a negative mental frame of mind (e.g., worried, fearful, angry).

But equally important is to develop the positive habit of being more conscious of the very process of taking in food—to be attentive and thankful as we eat. In fact, Cayce claimed that one's state of consciousness directly affects what will happen to the food being ingested. As he told his own son, Hugh Lynn Cayce, "That thou eatest, *see* it *doing* that *thou* would *have* it do. Now there is often considered as to why do those of either the vegetable, mineral, or combination compounds, have different effects under different conditions? It is the *consciousness* of the *individual body!*" (341-31) What a clear invitation to use the imaginative forces in a positive way as you are eating! "See it doing what you would have it do." For example, imagine your food bringing vitality and health to your entire body.

Of course, you may be thinking to yourself, "I'm too involved in conversation with other people during meal-

times. I can't spend all that time silently watching my attitudes and imagining good things happening with my
food." Obviously there are practical considerations when
it comes to creating this positive habit in your life. But as a
starting point, pick a meal each day—maybe a different
meal on different days—and take a moment for prayer or
to get yourself into the best frame of mind before you start
to eat. Whenever it's possible and practical during that
meal, spend even a few *seconds* to focus your attention on
imagining the positive effect that the food is having on
your body.

A Modern Day Success with This Positive Habit

Katherine was a forty-one-year-old mother of three children when she made a commitment to try the Three-Step
Body Tuneup for a month. Happily married, she also had a
career working full time as the manager of a busy lawyer
referral service. Katherine was the picture of a do-it-all
mom. She also had days, too, when she was the picture of
stress. Sometimes after a particularly busy day, she would
find that her left shoulder was very painful and tense.

The head-and-neck exercises were relatively easy for
her to incorporate into her daily routine. She would do
them when she woke and before retiring at night. There
were some awkward occurrences initially, however. She
wrote, "At first, when I came to the part that requires full
rotation, the most horrid noises could be heard as every
bone in my neck seemed to crunch and grind on the one in
front (or the one behind, I was not sure!) However, within
four to five days I could do a full rotation in either direction with greater ease, eventually being able to roll my
head around in silence!" Even better, she began to notice
that she no longer held tension in her shoulder muscles.
The head-and-neck exercises were a great benefit to her in
this regard.

Drinking eight glasses of water daily was a little harder for her to do regularly. As she put it, "Eight glasses of water is a lot of trips to the bathroom! Sometimes I found that instead of filling me up, as is suggested in many popular diets, it left me feeling very hungry." She found that it was easier to follow this positive habit at home since it wasn't as inconvenient as at work. At the office she found it embarrassing to be running to the ladies room twice as often as anyone else.

From the water drinking habit, some surprising results began to manifest. She found that if she started to feel irritable or short tempered, she would experience a craving to drink a glass of water. It had an immediate, calming effect that left her feeling good-humored. It was as if the water washed the negativity away. Another change made her start recognizing a distinct feeling when her body needed water. "I experience a kind of 'hunger,' not a thirst, and the only thing that satisfies the craving is to drink a glass of water. Being able to soothe one's temperament by drinking a glass of water must be one of the most overlooked benefits of all the Cayce material!"

However, like so many others, Katherine found it very difficult to eat consciously. She understood the ideas behind the positive habit and had hoped to be successful in visualizing how the food she ate would nourish her body to its highest good. "At first, as I would swallow a mouthful of food, I tried to 'see' it being absorbed into my blood stream, being carried to all my vital organs, enriching and nourishing every fiber of my being. From my hypnotherapy training I knew that the subconscious has no sense of humor and takes everything literally. This caused me some concern since I don't have sufficient knowledge of the workings of the human body to really know what each part should be doing."

She was concerned that she might be giving her body contradictory instructions and cause more harm than good.

The adjustment she decided to make was described this way. "It was taking her ages to actually get through a meal! So I decided that I would say a blanket blessing prior to each meal. The prayer went something like this: '*Dearest God, I give grateful thanks to you for the food that sits before me. I ask for a blessing upon each person who had a part in bringing this food to my table, and I ask that my physical body take only the nourishment that it needs and any excess or waste be swiftly eliminated through my body's normal means of doing this. Amen.'*"

It seemed to work for her, and she was able to enjoy her food in a timely manner while feeling that it was also being consumed consciously as she tried to really enjoy all the tastes before her. It even seemed to have a dramatic healing influence on a chronic health problem. "I had a remarkable success. I have suffered with irritable bowel syndrome for a number of years and yet I found that this simple blessing and paying attention to my food was all it took to eliminate attacks of this ailment completely. While prescription medications have their merits, they were invasive and the body comes to rely on them. This is the most powerful and beneficial remedy I have used and one I intend to continue. I feel quite sure that eventually my body will automatically come to respond to food in this manner, without the constant need to instruct it to do so."

A Story from the Cayce Archives

This story comes not from the archival records of the Cayce readings themselves but instead from the *research* archives—the reports of people who systematically have tried to apply what Cayce recommended, even though it is now decades after he stopped giving readings. As impressive as the individual case histories are—that is, the detailed reports of the people who got individual help from Cayce—perhaps even more significant are the archival records of large groups of people taking these ideas and putting them into application later. The help that is received by the latter group demonstrates how these principles about a spiritually centered and healthy life really do have wide applicability.

Many years after Cayce had died, a group of some 2000 people scattered across North America, made an effort to try the Three-Step Body Tuneup. The project was organized by the membership organization founded by Cayce in 1931, an organization that actually grew substantially in the years after his passing. These hundreds of members of the Association for Research and Enlightenment conducted the experiment from their own homes, and the required commitment was for only one week with the three steps, although many reported making them into three positive habits that would become part of their ongoing lifestyle.

Participants were reminded that there are no shortcuts to health and that they could hardly expect that one week of experimentation would work any miracle cures for ailments. Nevertheless, this project provided an opportunity for members to test, in an informal and small-scale way, three approaches for health tuneup mentioned in the Cayce readings. These three steps represented major areas of health-care strategy offered in the readings: (1) assimilations/eliminations, (2) exercise, and (3) attitudes. The exact methods they applied were the very same habits we've studied in this chapter.

Participants kept a daily log of their application of these procedures for seven days. More than 800 members—77 percent of them women—submitted report logs, many of them with accompanying letters, too. Those letters were almost entirely enthusiastic. (Admittedly, those who took time to apply these disciplines and complete the report form are most likely to be those who got helpful results, but less than half a dozen letters out of more than 300 ex-

pressed any form of disappointment from this project.)
Some comments referred to overall health improvements,
such as:

"My energy level was greatly increased. My sleep
patterns were improved—I seemed to sleep more pro-
ductively, not necessarily more. I seemed to awaken
more alert. I didn't need my usual caffeine to get going. I plan to adopt all three methods into daily life
because I'm so pleased with the results."

"I was doing [these procedures] already and it
works 1000 percent for me. I'm ninety-four and feel
like twenty-four!"

"I'm a tool and die maker and my work is very
stressful. [By] the end of the day and the end of the
work week, my energy level is very low. There was a
noticeable increase in my energy levels and overall
well-being. I was really surprised!"

Other comments made claims for rather specific and
dramatic changes, such as:

"Drinking six to eight glasses of water took out my
constipation so that my hemorrhoids seemed to dis-
appear suddenly. What a relief!"

"I had just had a cholesterol check [before the
project] and was surprised and scared at having a 303
level. Now I have it down to 275 and am still working
at it."

"I have chronic bursitis and received better relief
than with pain prescription."

"The neck-stretching exercises completely eliminated stiff necks which I had been having for some time. Also, I have not had my arms (forearms) go to sleep while sleeping, driving, typing, etc."

There were many anecdotal reports of how difficult the attentive eating proved to be, usually because of competing demands at the family table or because of life stresses. When it came time to indicate which of the procedures the participants planned to incorporate more permanently into their lifestyles, 92 percent indicated the head-and-neck exercise; 92 percent, the water drinking; and only 70 percent, the attentive eating. Overall, this informal research project strongly suggested that these positive habits are, in fact, ones that can be readily incorporated into one's lifestyle, especially if we're motivated to do it.

APPLYING THIS POSITIVE HABIT TO YOUR LIFE

Replicate in your own life the experiment conducted by these hundreds of people. Each day for a week, complete each part of the Three-Step Body Tuneup. Keep a journal record of how you feel from day to day. See if you notice any changes. The results are likely to be different from person to person; and, of course, it may be that a week won't be long enough to experience what this set of disciplines could do for you. But give it a try. Lots of people have noticed changes in even such a short time of implementing these positive habits.

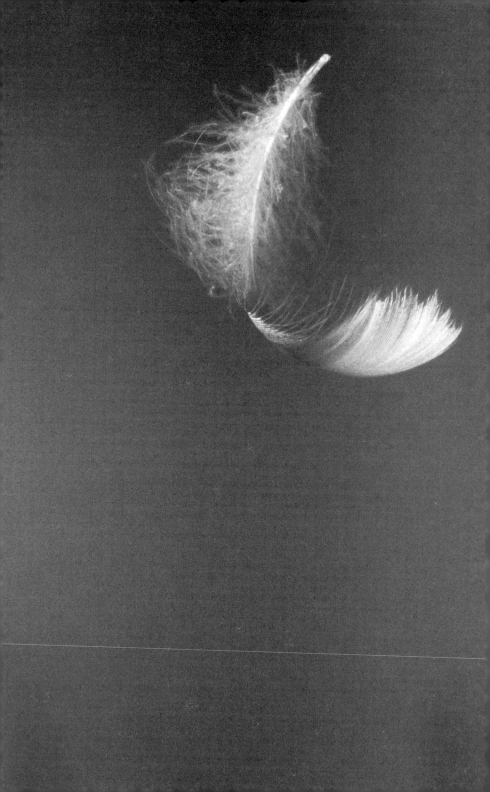

Positive
Habit
#12

Wrapping Up the Day: Bedtime Imaginative Recall

Many a night we barely make it to bed. Exhausted and stressed out from the demands of the day, we stumble to bed without any energy left. The oblivion of sleep is a welcome friend, a respite that will come none too soon.

Admittedly every bedtime is not going to be quite so desperate. But the fact remains: for most of us the day is full of so many diverse things to get done that we have little creative energy left by bedtime. The last hour of the day may often be spent passively in front of the television. In effect, we may waste the last moments of the day because we've seemingly used up our resources merely coping with the demands and expectations we've just waded through. Frequently, there just doesn't seem to be the focus needed to get anything very creative done—especially inner spiritual work.

Ironically, Edgar Cayce suggests that the last few waking minutes of a day provide a valuable opportunity for enhancing spiritual centeredness. In that very time period when we're most likely to feel inadequate or depleted, a special opportunity exists each evening. The positive habit is to carefully make use of the final two or three minutes of the day. By following a specific exercise, we not only can profoundly influence the quality of our sleep experience, we also affect the way we'll be able to meet challenges and stresses in the coming day.

In brief, this exercise involves a short review of the day's events. As we call to mind the most significant happenings—particularly in relation to other people—this imaginative exercise requires us to pay attention to something more than merely what took place. Of great importance is that we notice our own feelings and thoughts. But even more important is the ingredient to this exercise that gives it power: As we recall an event from the day, we try *to imagine what impact it had on the other people* who were involved. In other words, we imaginatively try to get inside the thoughts and feelings of the other person and experience the impact our own words or deeds may have had.

Think about how this positive habit might have worked for you if you had followed it last night at bedtime. You would have thought back over the day. Some of the experiences coming to mind would have been ones noticed by anyone who might have followed you around all day as an objective observer. Significant accomplishments, serious disagreements, stimulating opportunities, and new insights. Then you would have also asked yourself, "How did *other* people experience what was going on in these events?"

Next, you would have turned your attention to remembering the "little things" that had a big impact on your inner life for the day just ending. For example, it could have been something that someone said which deeply touched you, in a positive or a negative way. Or it could have been a change of mind or heart that suddenly happened during your day.

Many people find that it's easiest to do this exercise in *reverse chronology*—that is, starting with events at the end of the day and working back toward morning. They break the exercise into two parts: Phase 1, to pick the key events; then Phase 2, to go back over them more carefully one-by-one. But you'll be free to adapt this positive habit to a method that works best for you.

Here's what one person's reverse chronology list looked like on a weekend evening the first time he worked on this discipline:

- Talked with my wife about our different points of view regarding schedules for the upcoming week and about some financial decisions we face;
- Put the kids to bed;
- Talked on the phone long-distance with my brother;
- Played with my son and other kids at a birthday party for one of his friends;
- Fixed lunch for the family—everyone wanted something different;
- House cleaning and straightening with the kids;
- Breakfast with my daughter only because everyone else was sleeping in.

Feel free to review your day with forward chronology—from morning to evening—if that seems to work better for you. No matter which method you prefer, you'll probably get the most from this project if you *focus especially on your interactions with others* during the day. You can certainly include key moments from the day that happened to you privately. But as you see in the example above, pay special attention to interpersonal relations. That's particularly the arena in which challenges and soul-growth opportunities are present.

Of course, if all you do is make a list of events from the day, the most important ingredient of this positive habit is still missing. Now your attention needs to turn to the inner feelings or purposes involved in the events, plus your creative imaginings of how the other people were experiencing things. This second phase is the most significant part of the formula for how to end the day.

Once you are comfortably in bed and relaxed, you'll go back over the list in your mind for a deeper kind of analysis. For each key event of the day, do two steps. First review and relive the situation *as you experienced it at the time*. Try to notice your thoughts and feelings—and especially, your motives and purposes. Second, for those events that involved someone else, *imagine how that person experienced you and what happened.* In other words, what impact or effect did you have on that individual? Each of these imaginative experiences will probably take about ten seconds or so. For example, once this man made a brief list in his mind of half a dozen key events from his Saturday, he went back over them one by one.

What makes this positive habit work? To understand how something this simple could affect the night's sleeping experiences *and* the day ahead, we need to look carefully at the psychology of sleep and dreams. That theory is, in turn, deeply connected to the principle that ideals guide our lives. As potent motivators, ideals shape not only our waking life experiences but our nighttime ones as well. First, let's look at what Cayce suggests happens as we sleep, then at the role that ideals play in the process. Once we see how all this fits together, the value of his three-minute bedtime positive habit will be evident.

THE NATURE OF SLEEP

Sleep is a curious state. Although psychological and medical research knows far more now than it did in Cayce's time, our nocturnal levels of consciousness are still somewhat of a mystery. Esoteric psychologies, such as the one found in the Cayce readings, suggest some intriguing ideas that may be difficult for traditional research methods ever to test.

For example, Cayce indicated that sleep is akin to death. From a strictly physical point of view that makes sense. A sleeping person *looks* dead until we make a more careful examination. But from a spiritual angle this idea has more profound implications. As we view a sleeping person, we can't help but feel that "something" is missing—something has departed, call it the personality, soul, or spirit of the individual. Where has "it" gone? What does Cayce mean when he says that we leave the body at night as we fall asleep?

Cayce's psychology proposes that the sleep state provides the soul with a set of experiences somewhat like the ones that will be encountered in the future when the body actually dies. In other words, sleep is a shadow or metaphor of life after death.

We're left to wonder: What's it like after death? What happens? Cayce and many other esoteric philosophies offer a similar answer: the soul-mind reviews and digests the lessons of the life just completed. There were many lessons to learn in that lifetime, and they must be assimilated so that the soul can move on in its development.

But if sleep really is a preview of the after-death state, then it makes sense to suppose that a similar process happens in miniature each night. There is a review and an attempt to comprehend what has happened during the previous day. In this way of thinking, we might even look upon our dream experiences as preliminary efforts to prepare for a greater self-study that will eventually happen upon death. Dreams are a kind of small-scale reckoning that make it easier and more efficient to conclude a greater reckoning that is yet to come.

In a similar way, we might expect that the minutes spent just before falling asleep *could* be used to make sleeptime realizations easier and more efficient. What would happen if we tried to replicate *while still awake* the same *process* that would soon begin in the sleep and dream state? What might be the effect on our dream lives? And even more important: What might be the effect of this positive habit on our attitudes, moods, and physical health the next day?

To understand how this process works, let's go back to

the idea of one's soul-mind reviewing and digesting the lessons of recent experiences. What's involved in that review? The *ideals* of the soul are the most crucial element. When we leave the body—at death *or* at night upon falling asleep—the deepest ideals of the soul serve as a yardstick against which recent physical experiences are to be evaluated. It is our most cherished values and core belief that are at the heart of this inevitable self-review. The positive habit to make this bedtime review a *conscious* exercise at the end of the day simply makes it easier for us to learn the lessons of life and better cope with the new challenges that are coming the next day!

A Story from the Cayce Archives

Tom was struggling and he knew it. It was Christmas break, 1936, and just a year and a half into college at Virginia Polytechnic Institute his grades were miserable. He was at risk of flunking out. School had become a chore. When he was supposed to be studying for a test, all he could think about was getting outside and doing something active. It wasn't only on beautiful autumn afternoons that this restlessness would pull him away from his books. He never seemed to be able to concentrate for very long, even though he had a genuine interest in the subjects he was taking. And as his grades had begun to slide, the stress and tension had only increased, making his unsettled feelings grow.

His college career had begun with optimism and promise. His choice of Virginia Tech was principally because of advice from Edgar Cayce. During his senior year of high school he had received a reading from Cayce with all kinds of suggestions and recommendations for this life. Of course, it hadn't really been Tom's idea to get this psychic counseling from Cayce. It was his mother's.

Tom's mother was convinced that the mysterious man

from Virginia Beach had extraordinary powers to see into relationships, diagnose ailments of the body, and see into the future. He had been helpful to her, especially with her chronic spinal problems. And in her own readings from Cayce she had asked about her son and how she could insure his happiness. Cayce's answer to her had been simple and straightforward. It was now time for Tom to find his own way in life, to recognize his own ideals and goals. The most she could do was to provide influences that would help him stay in touch with the spiritual dimension of life and not get caught up in an imbalanced, materialistic view of life.

With her prodding, Tom had agreed to get his own reading from Cayce. He submitted questions that he formulated himself. High on his list had been his concerns about schooling and career. In that reading Cayce proposed a specific occupation for his life's work: a technical vocation that would specialize in pumps or in electrical mechanisms. What's more, Cayce psychically identified a specific college: Virginia Polytechnic Institute, just a half day's trip from his home in Washington, D.C.

The rest of the advice in that reading made enough sense to Tom that he decided to pursue Cayce's indications for schooling and field of study. He was accepted at Virginia Tech and enrolled in the autumn of 1935.

From the start, school had not been easy. His difficulties revolved around his inability to concentrate sufficiently. The course of study was demanding, with considerable reading every night. Most evenings Tom would end up cutting short his study time simply out of restlessness or nervous agitation. He had struggled through the first year's curriculum, barely getting by. But now, nearing the halfway point of his sophomore year, his inability to concentrate was about to get the best of him.

Arriving home for the holiday vacation, he was surprised to learn from his parents that Edgar Cayce would be visiting Washington, D.C. right after New Year's Day. One part of his mind felt a certain resentment toward Cayce. Following his advice to attend Virginia Tech was not turning out to look like a very smart decision. But another part of Tom—one that he knew was more honest and reliable— realized that he had only himself to blame for his problems at college. His mother in particular felt that more advice from Cayce would be the needed stimulant to help Tom get turned around with his school work. Principally because of his mother's strong faith in this psychic source of information, Tom agreed to accept further help from Cayce. His parents arranged for a second reading.

In early January 1937 Tom received from Cayce not just one but two psychic readings. The first was a lengthy discourse of mental and spiritual advice. The immediate follow-up reading was offered because of a surprising statement made by Cayce in the first of these two. In response to a question about why academic life at Virginia Tech was so difficult, Cayce gave an elaborate description of what was going on inside Tom. He was under constant stress at school. Those pressures were the same kind that virtually all college students feel, but Tom was having a particularly difficult time because something wasn't straight within himself.

The most pronounced condition creating this problem was in his physical body. Misalignments of the spine were causing pressures on the nervous system which, in turn, had an imbalancing effect on his endocrine glands and subsequently on his mental functioning. What was suffering most was his inability to concentrate normally. A general restlessness and lack of clear focus frequently took over.

Cayce prescribed specific treatments from an osteopathic physician and predicted that these procedures could make a big difference. It would put Tom back in touch with the best within himself—what Cayce called his "quieter self." That more authentic individuality had many extraordinary talents, just waiting to be expressed. Calling Tom to this bigger vision of his future, Cayce described how Tom had "often in its quieter self great imaginations, great abilities, great sense of justice, great sense of honor, integrity, sincerity. But to give expressions to these, it is almost as being short circuited by the very activities of the glandular system." (830-3)

However, the issues in need of change were more complex than merely physical. Equally important was the lack of adequate self-understanding and sufficient clarity about core values. Tom was soon to come to a crossroads in his life. In about three months he would have to make a choice about the direction for his life. There was sufficient time for the prescribed osteopathic adjustments to his spine to make a difference. But help from a skilled physician wasn't going to be enough. As he faced that crossroads, the decisions would require a deeper self-knowledge and self-understanding. For that reason Cayce gave a second set of recommendations for dealing with the stresses and uncertainties. Cayce's description of a particular positive habit related to daily life review began with this advice:

Each and every soul is meeting itself day by day. Everything we experience is potentially a lesson that will give an individual greater self-understanding. The best time to make a conscious effort to gain that new knowledge is at the end of the day. Just before going to sleep, take a few minutes to review the day. Ask yourself what have been your experiences throughout that whole day. You might even find it useful to write down what you observe. But this isn't to be a diary, and it certainly isn't for showing to anyone else. Instead, this positive habit for your inner growth is a daily exercise to help you recognize how you are changing. And within a month you are probably going to notice significant changes and growth in yourself.

As you're completing this end of the day review each night, notice from the day your desires and wishes, your deeds and acts of kindness. Remember the specific ways you were treated by others *and* how you responded. In all these efforts to review and learn, never be judgmental with yourself or someone else. The key is simply to recall, to observe carefully, and to learn about yourself.

Tom's parents saw to it that he followed through on the recommendation for osteopathic treatment. However, it's harder to say if the positive habit for the end of the day review was pursued diligently. Taking those two or three minutes in the evening is a private matter, and there are no records in the Cayce archives to indicate how seriously Tom may have taken the advice.

However, the files do tell the story of what followed in Tom's life. Some months later he decided to leave Virginia Tech. He decided to follow Cayce's advice concerning a career with mechanics, but he chose a less ambitious academic route and enrolled in mechanical school, specializing in aircraft engines. Upon graduation from technical school, he joined an airplane manufacturing firm. Soon thereafter he was married and started a family with his wife. He was successful in his chosen line of work and was eventually promoted to foreman.

We can well imagine that Tom's thoughts returned from time to time to the advice he had received from Cayce. No doubt there were times of stress in his adult life that were just as great as what he had experienced at college. The positive habit for an end-of-the-day review was meant to last a lifetime. In that simple exercise of looking back, one can make some sense out of the challenges of the day just gone by. Just two or three minutes wisely invested this way can profoundly change the way we'll feel about ourselves and the way we'll be ready to meet the new day just ahead.

A Modern Day Success with This Positive Habit

Cynthia was an at-home mother with two children and a

longtime interest in spirituality and metaphysics. For years she had participated in a small group that met weekly in her home town—a group of like-minded people who were committed to the disciplines of soul growth and staying spiritually centered.

One topic that the group frequently addressed was self-knowledge. Until we know and understand ourselves better, it's easy to be knocked off center by the vagaries of life. But with each step that we take along the path of "Know Thyself," as Edgar Cayce often put it, our capacity to be creative, vital, and centered becomes a little easier.

One stimulus to self-knowledge that was especially valuable for Cynthia was what happened each night in her soul mind as she would sleep—both her dreams and the unremembered intuitive reasoning that takes place as we sleep. She began to record her dreams regularly each morning, and Cynthia began seeing many patterns in her life, especially in regard to her emotional reactions to people and situations.

She discovered that it was particularly valuable to take this dream study for self-knowledge one step further: She added to her dream journal entries a record of her thoughts and feelings of the day just ended. Many nights there was a direct correlation between the day's happenings and the messages in her dreams. Writing her accounts of the day's events became an excellent way to unwind and reflect.

"Before I went to bed, I listed the main events and interactions of the day, usually starting with the end of the day and working backwards. After I listed those events, I contemplated their significance in the same way that I might look over the events and meaning of my whole life at the time of my death. I tried to see what I might like to change or pray about so that my next day would evidence the benefits of what I had learned."

She also experimented with keeping an even more careful record of various facets of her life experience. On a daily basis she evaluated her stress level, fulfillment level, whether or not she had meditated, her sleep soundness, and her feeling or mood upon awakening the next day.

After she had been keeping these notations for about a month, a situation arose and the end of the day review exercise proved to be particularly valuable. In describing the event that had seemingly knocked her off center, she wrote:

"Kelsey was a friend with whom I spent a great deal of time—walking, sharing interests in poetry, our children, music, and all sorts of things. I had learned from her about being playful with life and enjoying adventures exploring our city and meeting the eclectic variety of people she knew. She is curious about people and events and asks a lot of questions. I am more laid back and reluctant to disturb people. Today, however, I had not felt comfortable on our walk. I felt uneasy with Kelsey's critiques of the landscaping and roofs and paint jobs on the homes we passed. I didn't say anything, however. As I thought over what had happened that day (before I went to sleep), I decided that it would be unhealthy for me to continue our relationship the way it was. I asked to be guided to a new way of relating to Kelsey, if that were possible."

The end of the day review had provided Cynthia with the chance to stand aside from what had happened and invite her soul mind to discover a more creative way to deal with this difficulty—a situation that was almost sure to come up again with Kelsey.

That night Cynthia did not have a specific dream about Kelsey or their relationship. But she awoke the next morning with a strong sense of what needed to be done next. The only way she could change her interactions with her friend was to *speak up* about things she did not agree with. Just because she and Kelsey shared opinions on many topics, it still left room for them to disagree on other subjects. Cynthia awakened knowing that she needed to be more vocal in the relationship. She later wrote in her journal:

"The next day on our walk, when Kelsey was declaring how a particular yard should look, I asked her why that was so important to her, what was the big deal about how these people chose to present their home? She didn't really reply, but our talk shifted to discussions about what was really important to her, about her wanting courage to stand up for herself in family situations. In a way, I had taken on some of her role of asking questions and being more engaging, and I had also felt able to confront a situation that bothered me without being passive, snide, or aloof. For now at least, it seemed our friendship had the possibility of new dimensions of mutual joy."

For Cynthia this experiment had paid a big dividend. Even though it sometimes had seemed tedious to spend the last few minutes of the day reviewing her experiences, on this and on other occasions, it had allowed her to catch fresh insights on the patterns in her life and it had permitted a creative, problem-solving side of her mind to offer help.

Applying This Positive Habit to Your Life

Make a commitment for one week to this recommendation from Cayce for ending the day in a creative way. Each evening at bedtime think back over the day. Some of the experiences that come to mind will be ones noticed by anyone who might have followed you around all day as an objective observer. Significant accomplishments, serious disagreements, stimulating opportunities, and new insights. But just as easily, your bedtime recall will include "little things" that had a big impact on your inner life. Focus especially on your interactions with others during the day.

Then, once you are comfortably in bed and relaxed, go back over the list in your mind for a deeper kind of analysis. For each key event of the day, do two steps. First review and relive the situation as you experienced it at the time. Try to notice your thoughts and feelings—and especially, your motives and purposes. Second, for those events that involved someone else, imagine how that person experienced you and what happened. In other words, what impact or effect did you have on that individual?

Be alert for insights and self-knowledge that come directly from this end-of-the-day review. And also be alert for how this presleep mental work can have an impact on what happens in your mind overnight—either dreams that come *or* insights with which you awaken.

About Coauthor Mark Thurston

Mark Thurston, Ph.D., is an educator, researcher, and author who has served as a faculty member of Atlantic University for fifteen years, and has spent thirty-one years working in various capacities with A.R.E., including three years as co-executive director.

Mark's academic background is in psychology, and his special areas of expertise are transpersonal psychology and comparative spiritual philosophies. He is the author of eighteen books on various aspects of practical spirituality and transpersonal psychology. Among them are two books on dream work: *How to Interpret Your Dreams* and *Dreams: Tonight's Answers for Tomorrow's Questions.*

His most widely recognized writing has been in two areas:

(1) The field of human volition (that is, free will) with *Paradox of Free Will: Balancing Personal and Higher Will* and

(2) The field of vocation and life's work. Two books address methods by which the individual can find his or her most fulfilling life path: *Discovering Your Soul's Purpose* and *Soul Purpose: Discovering and Fulfilling Your Destiny.*

Among his most recent books are *The Essential Edgar Cayce, The Edgar Cayce Handbook for Creating Your Future* (coauthored with Chris Fazel), *Synchronicity as Spiritual Guidance,* and *Edgar Cayce's Guide to Spirituality for Busy People.*

As a teacher, Dr. Thurston's workshops, courses, and lectures are noted for their clarity and practicality. Over the last thirty years he has made presentations in more than 125 cities in the United States, in addition to presentations in seven other countries. He is executive producer and host of a twenty-six-part television series, *The New Millennium,* produced at PBS-affiliate WHRO in Norfolk, Virginia, and broadcast on the Wisdom Network. He is also cofounder of a nonprofit educational organization that focuses on small group workshop courses to foster self-understanding, change, and courage—The Personal Transformation and Courage Institute—whose programs are described online at www.soul-purpose.com/courage.

A.R.E. PRESS

The A.R.E. Press publishes books, videos, and audio-tapes meant to improve the quality of our readers' lives—personally, professionally, and spiritually. We hope our products support your endeavors to realize your career potential, to enhance your relationships, to improve your health, and to encourage you to make the changes necessary to live a loving, joyful, and fulfilling life.

For more information or to receive a free catalog, call:

1-800-723-1112

Or write:

A.R.E. Press
215 67th Street
Virginia Beach, VA 23451-2061